SUPER CHEAP TOKYO

The Ultimate Budget Travel Guide to Tokyo and
the Kanto Region

Matthew Baxter

Share yourself with the book and win prizes!

Why not share your amazing journey across Japan with your friends by posting a picture on Facebook, Twitter or Instagram? Just include the book (or cover) in the photo and mention @SuperCheapJapan for your chance to win! Monthly prizes will be up for grabs, such as festival tickets, gift vouchers, free stays and much more.

Help spread the word!

Please help the book by writing a review on the website where you bought the book, sharing the book on Facebook or Twitter, or telling a friend. As this is a self-funded indie project, it would be super useful and very much appreciated! It will also allow me to continue to write more budget travel books about this amazing country. Doumo arigatou!

Like or follow us to get the latest tips and deals

Join us on Facebook at https://www.facebook.com/supercheapjapan or follow us on Twitter at https://twitter.com/SuperCheapJapan to receive information on new discounts, the latest deals, cherry blossom forecasts and interesting budget travel reports. You can also get all the latest info at http://www.supercheapjapan.com/.

Super Cheap Japan
9 Eashing Lane
Godalming, Surrey GU7 2JZ
www.supercheapjapan.com/contact/

Book Layout ©2018 BookDesignTemplates.com

Ordering Information:
Special discounts are available on quantity purchases by corporations, associations, and others. For details, contact the "Special Sales Department" at the address above.

Super Cheap Tokyo: The Ultimate Budget Travel Guide to Tokyo and the Kanto Region / Matthew Baxter - 1st ed.
Paperback ISBN 978-1-9998100-5-4
Ebook ISBN 978-1-9998100-6-1

Contents

Welcome to Tokyo

Kaminarimon, leading up to Senso-ji Temple in Asakusa, Tokyo

Welcome to Tokyo, capital city of Japan and one of the most exciting cities in the world. More than 13 million people live here, while the greater Tokyo metropolis houses over 35 million. With such a large population and a diverse variety of areas, Tokyo is known as a 'city of cities'. From geeky hotspots such as Akihabara, to quiet and tranquil gardens such as Kiyosumi Garden, to the bright lights of the skyscrapers of Shinjuku, Tokyo has it all.

A very favorable exchange rate has allowed Tokyo to blossom for budget travelers. While an average hostel room would have cost around $50 in 2012, it now costs around $30. A cheap meal starts at around $5, while it would have cost about $8.50 several years ago. There are also 100-yen ($1) stores, beds from under $10 a night and countless cheap restaurants for tourists to enjoy. With a cheap subway network and many discounts passes, those in the know can have both an affordable and supremely exciting holiday in Tokyo.

With all that there is to see, it's recommended to start by heading to the highlights, then explore some of the less touristy spots nearby. This book has been designed in a way that allows you to both see the best sights in Tokyo, as well as off-the-beaten track experiences, all while keeping costs low.

A little bit of history

Tokyo is a relatively new capital. In 1590 the Shoguns, Japan's military dictators, moved from Kyoto to Edo, the old name for Tokyo. While the emperor stayed in Kyoto, the real power and money moved to the new city. In the early 17th century, Edo blossomed under Shogun Tokugawa Ieyasu and spread out around Edo Castle. The Shogunate finally fell in 1867, bringing Emperor Meiji into power. He opened up the country, allowing foreign culture and technology, particularly from the west, to enter the country via ports such as Yokohama.

In 1923, Tokyo was devastated by the Great Kanto Earthquake. More than 2 million people were left homeless and more than 100,000 perished. The city was further damaged by the bombing in World War Two, which destroyed much of the capital. Thankfully the city experienced rapid growth after the war and has rebuilt itself into a real powerhouse.

How to save on your holiday with this book

Things to do

This book will show you how to have an amazing holiday in Japan without blowing a hole in your pocket. You'll be shown plenty of options for free things to do in each location, as well as information on discounts or free samples. Try to do the cheaper or free activities first, then if you have enough time or feel you need to do more, try the more expensive things in the area.

Sample itineraries and discount passes

If you are a bit stuck, there are plenty of sample itineraries for subway or train passes, which will help to ease planning. Info on discount passes for each area will also help you to save big!

Budget food

Tokyo is full of budget restaurants and takeaway joints. These are included on the maps, as well as in the Budget Food sections, as they can be tricky to find if you're not a local. Don't forget to consider buying food from supermarkets or convenience stores, especially in the evening when prices are often slashed to get rid of stock. Nothing better than super cheap sushi in the evening! They are also good for drinking, as it's perfectly legal here to buy a beer and drink in public.

Most of the budget restaurants have water jugs to refill your bottle, and other spots to refill, such as from water fountains in parks, have also been included. The 100-yen shops (around $1) are also listed, as you can buy almost anything, from microwavable curry to essential travel items. Japanese pharmacies and drug stores often have even cheaper prices for drinks and snacks as well. Buying a large bottled drink in a 100-yen shop, then using the bottle for the rest of your trip is a great way to save on money. Tap water is drinkable.

How to use the maps

As most of Tokyo's streets don't have names, detailed instructions for getting to places, and simple maps when appropriate, are provided so you won't spend time and money getting lost. You'll never need to get an expensive taxi. Use landmarks on the maps to help, too, and save on transportation by using the recommended walking routes.

Map Legend

- Convenience store
- Cheap supermarket
- 100 yen store
- Pharmacy
- Tourist information
- Recommended walking route
- Budget accommodation
- Post office

Free wifi locations

Most of the tourist spots in Tokyo are pretty well connected up to wifi these days. There is really no need to buy expensive rental phones or wireless internet adapters for the phone networks because of this. In the rare case that wifi is difficult to find, wifi location information is included in this book.

Map of central Tokyo

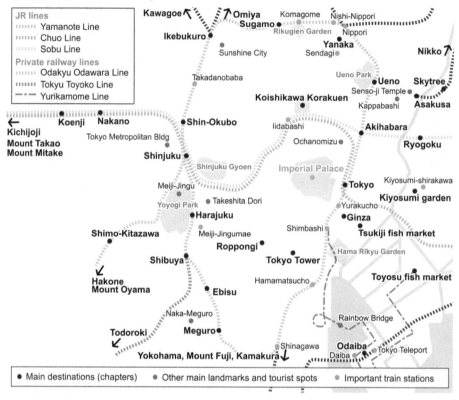

JR lines
- Yamanote Line
- Chuo Line
- Sobu Line

Private railway lines
- Odakyu Odawara Line
- Tokyu Toyoko Line
- Yurikamome Line

● Main destinations (chapters)   ● Other main landmarks and tourist spots   ● Important train stations

Tokyo Top 10 Spots

1) Shinjuku

Tokyo's best cosmopolitan spot, Shinjuku is fall of budget superstores, great low-cost food and a high number of tax-free shops. It also has a huge park and is a good transportation hub for going off to sights on the west side of Tokyo.

2) Harajuku

Tokyo's best spot for all things kawaii (cute). Cheap clothes, accessories and some amazing trendsetting fashion from the locals. The main streets can get pretty busy, but if you head down the smaller alleyways, you're sure to find some surprises!

3) Asakusa

The tourism center of Tokyo, and an essential stop for first-timers to Tokyo. It can feel too touristy at points, but the iconic temples such as Senso-ji Temple and a bustling market help to create an awesome atmosphere.

4) Ueno

A huge park with a host of free temples and shrines to visit, plus a busy, down-to-earth downtown full of enthusiastic street sellers. In addition, it's the place to come in Tokyo if you want to see pandas (at Ueno Zoo). Truly Tokyo.

5) Shibuya
Featuring Tokyo's most photographed area, the Shibuya Pedestrian Scramble, this hyperactive area has lots of people watching and window shopping opportunities for budget travelers.

6) Akihabara
The geek capital of Tokyo, if not the world. All kinds of geeky delights here, from maid cafes to computer megastores. Also the perfect spot for a bit of tax-free electronics and videogame shopping.

7) Tokyo Metropolitan Observation Decks
Skip the pricey Skytree and head to this free observation deck for a spectacular view over the city. On a clear day, it's possible to see the stunningly snowcapped Mount Fuji in the distance, in addition to the whole city and surrounding mountains.

8) Shimo-Kitazawa
A maze of narrow streets, that look completely unchanged from the 1950s or 1960s. No ugly skyscrapers here, just a super cool town to explore.

9) Yanaka
Worth a visit, especially if you have already done most things in Tokyo, Yanaka is a quieter tourist area than most. Not as commercialized as others, it has a very authentic atmosphere.

10) Koenji
Another hip area, Koenji is full of fascinating antique shops, used goods stores and cool cafes. Plus super cheap pizzas for under 400 yen!

When to go to Tokyo

Tokyo is a big city, with lots to do any time of the year.

Spring (March to May)
It's cherry blossom season! An amazing time to come. Just be sure to book as soon as you can so you don't get stuck with expensive hotels. You can also head out to places such as Nikko to see the sakura in quieter surroundings. Get the latest forecasts at www.supercheapjapan.com.

Summer (June to August)
Tokyo can get very hot and humid this time of year, but there are lots of free festivals to enjoy. If it gets too much, just relax inside one of the countless air-conditioned convenience stores and grab a cheap drink.

Fall/Autumn (September to November)
With more manageable temperatures, the fall is a great time to visit Japan's capital. Tokyo also has a good number of spots for the autumn leaves, which in terms of timing are easier to catch than the cherry blossoms. Be sure to check www.supercheapjapan.com for this year's timings.

Winter (December to February)
Tokyo has some amazing illuminations this time of year, especially in Shinjuku and Roppongi. They are a great, free activity. While some places can be closed, you'll never be far away from somewhere still open.

Peak seasons to avoid
If you can, try to avoid Golden Week (April 29th to May 5th), Obon holidays (around August 13th to 16th) and around the New Year holidays, when prices can go up quite a lot.

Free festivals in Tokyo

January
6th Dezome-shiki, Odaiba: Firemen show off their machines and do various stunts.

February
From mid-February Ume Matsuri, Ueno: Amazing plum festival at Yushima Tenmangu Shrine.

March
The cherry blossoms are out! See the Cherry Blossom guide below for where to go.

April
Second to third Sundays Kamakura Festival, Kamakura: Ritual dance performances based on the samurai of medieval Japan.

May
The Saturday and Sunday closest to May 15th Kanda Matsuri, Kanda: One of Tokyo's top three festivals. We go every year.
18th Shunki Reitaisai, Nikko: Grand procession of 1,000 'samurai warriors' through the town.
Third Sunday and preceding Friday and Saturday Asakusa Sanja Matsuri, Asakusa: Amazing portable shrines are paraded throughout the town. Mind-blowing stuff.
Closest weekend to May 28th Hanazono Shrine Grand Festival, Shinjuku: Featuring ceremonial rites and dances, plus some cheap food stalls. On the Sunday, a huge 1.5 ton portable shrine (mikoshi) is taken on a tour of the surrounding neighborhoods.

June
Mid-June Sanno Matsuri, central Tokyo: Another big festival in Tokyo, with a splendid procession of miniature shrines.

July
Last Saturday Sumida River Fireworks, Asakusa: Tokyo's biggest and best fireworks display.

August
Early to mid-August Asagaya Tanabata Matsuri Festival, near Koenji: Colorful bamboo and paper decorations fill up this lovely shopping street in Asagaya.
Late August Awa-odori, Koenji: Awa-odori consists of nearly 200 Japanese dance groups showing off some spectacular traditional dances and music from across the country.
Last weekend Omotesando Genki Festival, Harajuku: One of the largest festivals in Tokyo, it has more than 5000 energetic dancers from 100-plus groups performing.

September
14-16th Reitaisai, Kamakura: Traditional horseback archery display and contest.

October
Late October to mid-November Kongo-ji Temple Chrysanthemum Festival, Takahata-Fudoson Temple: More than 1500 varieties of flowers on display, from Bonsai to colorful cascades.
Mid-October Tokyo Yosakoi Festival, Ikebukuro: Countless groups showing off this energetic, yet very traditional form of Japanese dance.

November
3rd Hakone Daimyo Gyoretsu, Hakone: Around 200 people in samurai warrior and Japanese princess costumes parade around the hot spring town.

December
Christmas and New Year Lights Terrace City, Shinjuku and Roppongi Midtown, Roppongi.

Tax-free shopping

Japan has a sales tax of 8%, going up to 10% in the future, but those with a tourist visa are eligible for tax-free shopping. With a great exchange rate for most travelers and tax-free shopping, there has never been a better time to shop here. Almost all the shops here are proudly showing off their tax-free status with huge signs and in-store announcements.

How to do tax-free shopping in Japan

All you need to do in the shop is show your passport and the tax will be taken off when you purchase. Some naughty shops levy a charge to get tax-free, so avoid these if it's mentioned.

Consumables (foods, drinks, medicines, cosmetics...)
Must be purchased at the same store on the same day, and the total spending must be more than 5000 yen. Items must be taken out of Japan within 30 days of purchase.

Non-consumables (electric appliances, clothing, accessories...)
Must be purchased at the same store on the same day, and the total spending must be more than 5000 yen. Items must be taken out of Japan within six months of purchase.

At the airport
Be sure to keep the receipt you get when you buy your tax-free items. As you go through customs after checking in for your flight, there will be a counter where you have to show this. Have the items ready to show, just in case they ask, as you may be asked to pay tax for a consumable item if you have already consumed it in Japan and cannot show it at the airport.

Top 3 tax-free hotspots in Tokyo

Ginza
While it has a high-end reputation, these days there is an increasing number of lower end brands here, as well as smaller shops selling real bargains on travel items.

Shinjuku
As would be expected for the largest metropolitan area, Shinjuku has many large stores, with branches from all the main clothing, electronic and travel brands.

Akihabara
The place to fill up on tax-free electronics, videogames, figurines, anime and manga.

Cherry blossom viewing (花見)

Yanaka-reien Cemetery in Yanaka, east Tokyo

With countless places to see the cherry blossoms and a great transportation network, Tokyo and the surrounding Kanto area are great choices. From local gardens to shopping streets, you will never be more than a few minutes away from a sakura (cherry blossom) tree. They provide a perfect spot for a cheap meal or drink, as the tradition is to grab some cheap grub and beers from a nearby convenience store and enjoy them under the pink and white trees. For Tokyo, first bloom is usually around 22nd March, while full bloom is around 30th March.

Top 5 spots for cherry blossoms

1) Ueno Park
The biggest park in Tokyo for cherry blossoms, and it's all free. Can get super busy, but all the small stalls selling cheap food are a real plus.

2) Sumida Park
Along Sumida river in Asakusa. A fun, party atmosphere fills the park, which has a varied selection of cherry blossom trees.

3) Meguro River
A short walk from Meguro, the main action is around Naka-Meguro. This long, winding river is the coolest place to see the cherry blossoms, as it's lined with hip cafes and clothing shops. Come in the night with a beer or two from a convenience store.

4) Imperial Palace East Garden
Gets busy but has a host of different sakura trees to enjoy. It's also worth walking around the palace, in particular outside the British embassy, near Hanzomon on the Hanzomon Line.

5) Hachiman Shrine
See the big Buddha hanging out with all the cherry blossom trees in Kamakura. The grand, wide road leading up to the temple is lined with cherry blossoms.

Discount transportation passes

Tokyo has three main networks: Tokyo Metro (main subway network), Toei Subway (only four lines) and JR (national rail) trains. Passes are a great way to save a bit of cash when doing a lot in one day, and also give extra flexibility to try somewhere new if you have a bit of free time. The pass you choose really depends on where you want to visit, so check the 'Recommended rail passes' for each place. The easiest way is to get the Tokyo Subway Ticket on the first day, then see how much you can get done on that.

At the time of writing, the one-day passes for the subway networks also come with a 'Chikatoku' discount booklet, which allows pass owners to get discounts or free bonus items at more than 400 locations in Tokyo. See http://chikatoku.enjoytokyo.jp/en/ for the full list.

There are also discount train passes for many of the side trips outside Tokyo. Information on these and the discounts they offer are detailed in the relevant destination page.

Tokyo Subway Ticket 24h/48h/72h
Only available to tourists, so you need to show a passport or proof of address when purchasing. This awesome ticket allows use of both Toei Subway and Tokyo Metro. Available at Haneda or Narita Airport, or some Bic Camera or Laox Tax Free shops. See http://www.tokyometro.jp/en/ticket/value/travel/ for more locations. *24 hours: Adults 800 yen, children 400 yen. 48 hours: Adults 1200 yen, children 600 yen. 72 hours: Adults 1500 yen, children 750 yen*

Tokyo Metro 24-hour Ticket
If you have no need to also use the Toei Subway, then get this pass instead, and save a few hundred yen. This may require longer journey times to some destinations, but it's the cheapest way to get around the city. *Adults 600 yen, children 300 yen*

Tokyo Metropolitan District Pass (Tokunai Pass)
A good option if you are going to main transportation hubs like Akihabara, Shibuya, Tokyo or Shinjuku stations or want to venture a little into the suburbs, such as to Koenji or Nakano. This pass allows unlimited use of JR trains only, and includes all their trains in central Tokyo, plus a little distance outside. Available at all JR stations in central Tokyo. *Adults 750 yen, children 370 yen*

Sample day itineraries

Cool Tokyo (Tokyo Metro 24-hour Ticket)
First head to Harajuku to see what's trending in everything kawaii (cute fashion), before dropping into Shibuya to see Japan's top brands. After lunch, geek out in Akihabara and visit Asakusa for Tokyo's most popular temple. Then head to Koenji for a more down-to-earth vibe.

Tradition and history in Tokyo (Tokyo Subway Ticket)
First go to Ryogoku to visit the free Sumo museum and then the Edo-Tokyo museum, to learn all about Tokyo's history. After lunch head to Kiyosumi Garden to see a traditional Japanese garden in all its glory. If you have time left, head to Yanaka to see what an old-style neighborhood looks like.

The big, big city (Tokyo Metropolitan District Pass)
Start in Shinjuku, where you can go up the observation tower to get a view over the city and see the huge Shinjuku Gyoen park. After lunch, proceed to Shibuya for some photo taking, especially of the super busy pedestrian crossing. Head east for the Imperial gardens and views of the classically designed Tokyo station. Finally head to Sugamo for some discount shopping and relax in the local hot spring.

Getting to and around Tokyo

How to get there and away

By air
There are two main airports for Tokyo, Narita Airport (NRT) and Haneda Airport (HND). Both offer cheap ways to get into the city, so it doesn't matter too much which one you use.

Narita Airport transportation
Access Narita (1000 yen per trip, kids half price) and Keisei (1000 yen one-way, 1900 yen return) both offer regular buses into the city. Also consider using the Keisei local and express line trains to/from Nippori station in Tokyo (80 mins, 1030 yen). The Narita Express and Keisei Skyliner trains approximately double the prices, and don't save you that much time.

Haneda Airport transportation
Haneda is much closer to downtown Tokyo, so it's cheap and easy just to use the Keikyu Line or Monorail. Take the Keikyu Line to Shinagawa (16 mins, 410 yen) or the Monorail to Hamamatsucho (20 mins, 490 yen), then transfer from these central hubs.

By train
If you are far from Tokyo and have the Japan Rail Pass, you should take the Shinkansen to Tokyo or Shinagawa station. Otherwise, trains are often too pricey.

By bus
If you are traveling far from Tokyo, such as from Kyoto, Osaka or Hiroshima, and don't have a Japan Rail Pass then it's much, much cheaper to take the bus. Check prices at Japan Bus Lines, Willer Bus and JR Bus Kanto.

Volunteer guides and free tours

Tokyo International Student Guide (https://www.facebook.com/tsgg.for.tourists/) are a bunch of friendly students who are eager to show tourists around. Tokyo SGG Club (http://tokyosgg.jp/guide.html) are more focused on the east side, such as the museum, parks and shrines around Asakusa and Ueno. No reservation is required, just head to the information center in Asakusa and see what's on. Tokyo Free Guide (http://www.tokyofreeguide.org/) are another group worth considering. If these groups cannot be of help, have a look at https://www.jnto.go.jp/eng/arrange/travel/guide/guideservice.html for an official list of more volunteer groups.

Had a great time with one of the guides? Show your appreciation by posting on Twitter or Facebook, especially on the groups page. Please mention @SuperCheapJapan to let us know!

Grutto Pass (ぐるっとパス)

For most budget travelers wanting to visit a gallery or two, the latest listings on TimeOut Tokyo are worth checking out (many are free). But for real gallery and museum junkies, the Grutto Pass should be considered. Unlike many countries, most museums in Japan charge entry fees, so costs can add up. The Grutto Pass provides free admission or discounts for two months to 92 art galleries, museums, zoos and more. If you want to visit many museums and galleries in Tokyo, you will really start to save some money. See how much you could save at the official website (http://www.rekibun.or.jp/grutto/english.html). *2200 yen. Note that there is also a Tokyo Metro & Grutto Pass, which also includes two days of subway travel for 2870 yen.*

How to get around Tokyo

Using the train or subway is the easiest way to get around Tokyo. When not using a discount pass, most people use the main IC card in Tokyo, the Suica card, which is available to buy at any ticket machine from a JR station in Tokyo. The Metro network also offers a card called Pasmo, which has similar features. Journey prices are a little cheaper when using the cards, so if you are in Tokyo for more than a few days then you can save a bit. They also reduce the chance of overpaying when transferring between lines, which can be confusing. The Suica and Pasmo card networks are now interchangeable in central Tokyo. City fares in this book show the IC card price. *1000 yen (500 yen deposit, 500 yen put on card)*

Tokyo Metro and Toei Subway – major stations and interchanges

The official subway map can be quite overwhelming for some tourists, so here is a mini-map to help getting around the network easier. This simplified map just shows all the subway stops you will need to use in this book, as well as necessary interchanges. To reach stops not in this book, just use the free Tokyo Subway Navigation app or one of the maps inside any station.

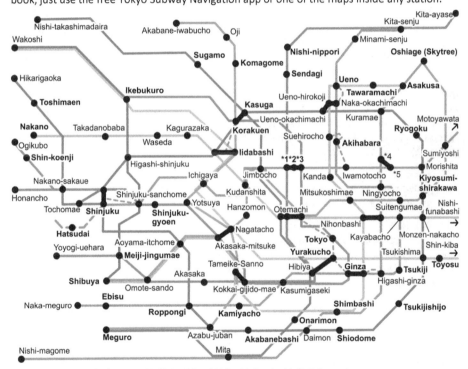

*1: Shin-Ochanomizu *2: Ogawamachi *3: Awajicho *4: Higashi-nihombashi *5: Bakuro-yokoyama

	Tokyo Metro lines		Toei Subway lines
● Major subway station (bold)	═══ Marunouchi Line	═══ Hanzomon Line	═══ Oedo Line
● Other subway station	═══ Tozai Line	═══ Hibiya Line	═══ Shinjuku Line
●━━● Major interchange	═══ Yurakucho Line	═══ Ginza Line	═══ Asakusa Line
- - - Short walk between stations	═══ Fukutoshin Line	═══ Chiyoda Line	═══ Mita Line
	═══ Namboku Line	═══ Keio New Line (not covered by passes)	

Things to know before you visit Tokyo

While traveling in Tokyo can be more expensive than a lot of Asian cities, the well integrated, cheap subway network and countless cheap restaurants should help to keep costs down. Use the costs here as a rough guide to what you'll be spending.

Exchange rates
These are the rates as of August 2018. Check www.supercheapjapan.com for the latest rates. 1 US Dollar = 111 yen • 1 Euro = 130 yen • 1 British Pound = 146 yen • 1 Canadian Dollar = 84 yen • 1 Australian Dollar = 82 yen

Average daily costs for budget travelers
Single Traveler: 6000-8000 yen • Multiple travelers: 4000-5000 yen per person

Usual prices
Dorm bed: 2500-3500 yen • Budget eat-in meal: 390-600 yen • Convenience store meal: 290-500 yen • Cup noodles: 100-190 yen • Subway ticket: 165-195 yen

Money
Tokyo is the most modern city in Japan, but it is still essential to have cash on you at all times. Most restaurants will not accept credit cards, but an increasing number accept IC cards, such as the Suica or Pasmo train cards. As with the rest of Japan, tipping is frowned upon. Great!

Electricity
Tokyo has an electrical current of 100v, 50Hz. Most devices such as phones and laptops will work fine, but appliances such as hair dryers and shavers can work slowly or may even get damaged without an adapter. Visitors from the UK and Europe will probably need to get an adapter anyway, but those from North America may sometimes be fine as the shapes of the pins are identical. You can buy a cheap adapter at the airport or in any large electronics store.

Visas
Japan allows visa free travel from most countries for tourists, but make sure you check with the Japanese embassy where you live. Working holiday visas are also worth considering.

Coin lockers (コインロッカー)
Lockers are available at almost every station in Tokyo, and most in the Kanto area around the capital. They are easy to use, and often have English instructions. If you arrive somewhere early, it may be cheaper and more time efficient to put your luggage in a locker and check out the sights before checking in at your accommodation.

Best free apps to download before you go

- Skyscanner for comparing cheap airplane tickets.
- Google Translate, then download the Japanese language pack in the app for offline use. Also translates text only using your phone camera. Great when trying to decipher Japanese menus!
- Japan Connected-Free Wifi, to easily find free wifi spots nationwide.
- Tokyo Subway Navigation, the official app for navigating the Tokyo Metro. Usable offline.
- Booking.com to quickly cancel or amend bookings. Airbnb is also worth downloading.
- Google Maps and Maps.me, then in Maps.me download the areas you will be visiting.
- XE Currency for comparing prices to back home.
- Splittr, which allows you to see who owes what to who when traveling with friends.
- The Time Out app has the latest listings for live events, new exhibitions and local festivals.

West Tokyo

Shinjuku (新宿)

Shinjuku Gyoen in autumn

A great place to start your adventures in Japan, Shinjuku is the main business and entertainment district in Tokyo. While Shibuya is well and truly aimed at younger people, Shinjuku is a bit more sophisticated than its southern brother. It's therefore a great place to introduce yourself to that Japanese mix of old and new.

A little bit of history

While many people have an image of Tokyo being completely full of skyscrapers, this is in fact not the case, with the city having several pockets of skyscraper districts. In 1923, when the Great Kanto earthquake obliterated most of Tokyo, west Shinjuku was left relatively unscathed due to its seismically stable location. It therefore developed as a business district, full of grand skyscrapers. In the following years, most of Tokyo was destroyed by air raids in World War Two, but the pre-war form of Shinjuku was retained to ease reconstruction, with the exception of Kabukicho. There are still therefore plenty of interesting narrow streets to explore, and a short walk will get visitors away from all the commercial activity.

Things to do

Tokyo Metropolitan Observation Decks (東京都庁)

The free Tokyo Metropolitan Government Office offers great views of the city during daytime and evening, plus on clear days you can even see Mount Fuji. You can also buy your name in Japanese characters in the gift shop at the top. Save on the cost of the expensive Skytree and visit here instead! *FREE • 9:30am-11pm (entry ends 30 minutes before closing) • On foot: Walk west for 10 minutes from Shinjuku station in the underground passageway to Tochomae station, then continue five minutes west. By subway: Take the Toei Oedo Line from Shinjuku station to Tochomae station (2 mins, 174 yen). By bus: Shinjuku Washington Hotel stop (WE Bus)*

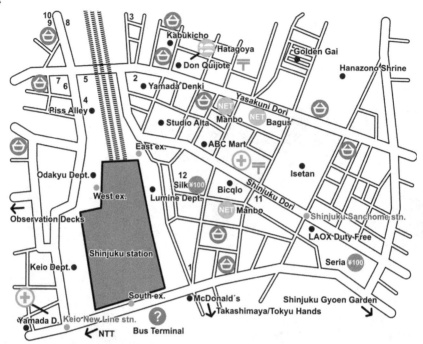

Shinjuku Gyoen Garden (新宿御苑)

Usually a must see for any visitor to Tokyo, Shinjuku Gyoen Garden is a large, feature-full park next to Shinjuku station. The garden was previously the mansion grounds of the Naito family, feudal lords in the Edo period. Every visitor makes a trip here when coming to Shinjuku, but as this garden is so large and varied it never seems overcrowded. In addition to the traditional Japanese garden and small pavilion, there are French and English inspired gardens, a small forest with Japanese cedar trees and a brand new, ultra-modern greenhouse. *Adults 200 yen, Children 50 yen • 9am-4pm • On Foot: From Shinjuku station, make your way to Bicqlo (ビックロ). Walk east (past Isetan Department Store), down Shinjuku Dori (street) until you get to Sekaido stationery shop (世界堂), then turn right and walk down for the entrance. By subway: Take the Metro Marunouchi Line from Shinjuku to Shinjuku-gyoenmae (2 mins, 165 yen). By bus: Shinjuku Gyoen stop (WE Bus)*

Hanazono Shrine (花園神社)

Lovely respite from the chaos of Shinjuku, a cool place to chill out and have a bento or snack. Hanazono is a Shinto shrine founded in the 17th century and is considered to be one of the most important in Tokyo by locals, which explains why it's still there with all the huge concrete buildings around it. The shrine has become a favorite for local businessmen to pray for business success and prosperity. *FREE • 24h • On foot: Walk down Shinjuku Dori, take a left after Isetan Department Store and walk down (total 15 mins). By subway: Shinjuku-Sanchome exit E2. By bus: Shinjuku Oiwake stop (WE Bus)*

Kabukicho (歌舞伎町)

Tokyo's, and Japan's, most famous red light district. For budget travelers, it's a fascinating walk around, taking in all the bright lights, watching the nightclub and bar hosts and hostesses getting up to their business. It's generally recommended to stay away from bars and restaurants here, as prices are generally high and foreigners have been known to be overcharged. Just bring your camera after dark and take it all in. *Just outside Shinjuku station, take the east exit and walk towards Seibu Shinjuku station, right next to Kabukicho*

NTT InterCommunication Center (NTT インターコミュニケーション・センター)

Free media, art and communications gallery in Nishi-Shinjuku, the skyscraper district. NTT is Japan's main telephone provider, and this museum was started to commemorate the 100th anniversary of telephones in Japan. The museum has an excellent selection of innovative, fun and thought-provoking art and multimedia pieces, and shows off some amazing new artists. *FREE (extra for special exhibitions, which are FREE with Grutto Pass) • 11am-6pm • On foot: Near the Keio New Line station. Walk along the main road (Shinjuku dori) in the opposite direction of the bridge and Bus Terminal. By subway: From Shinjuku, take the Keio New Line to Hatsudai station (1 min, 124 yen). By bus: Shinjuku Washington Hotel stop (WE bus)*

Volunteer guides and tours

The tourist information center in the Tokyo Metropolitan Building (see above) can organize free volunteer tours in English.

Getting around

Once you are at Shinjuku station, everywhere is within walking distance if you don't mind walking for 5-15 minutes to get between tourist spots. The shops around the station are also close, taking only a few minutes between each one. There are two main streets, Shinjuku Dori to the south and Yasukuni Dori to the north. But be warned! Shinjuku station is a complete maze and even for people that have worked there for years, it can be easy to get lost. Use the in-station signs to get to one of the above shops or tourist sites if you are completely lost, from where you can get your bearings.

Transportation passes and discounts

There is also a bus service called WE Bus (新宿 WE バス) that takes riders around the main spots listed above, from 7am-6pm (100 yen each ride, 300 yen for day pass). Tickets and passes available on the bus, with the most useful route being the Shinjuku Gyoen + Nishi-Shinjuku Route. Starting at the Shinjuku Bus Terminal near Shinjuku station, south exit is recommended, to avoid traipsing around the huge station looking for the right bus stop.

Budget food

Around the station (east side)

There are so many cheap restaurants around Shinjuku (usually with English menus), we would actually recommend strolling around this fascinating metropolis and seeing what takes your fancy. Here are some of the highlights if you are too hungry to walk around!

1) Senka Soba (千曲そば) - Various styles of simple soba and udon. *Soba from 250 yen • 24h • From the south-east exit, take the wide stairs down and walk ahead, it's on the corner*

2) Yoshinoya (吉野家) - Gyudon eat-in and takeaway. *Meals from 330 yen • 24h • Next to Yamada Denki (LABI) on Yasukuni Dori*

3) Hidakaya (日高屋) - Tokyo's super cheap ramen chain. Fried rice and gyoza dumplings also available. *Ramen from 390 yen • 24h • Opposite Seibu-Shinjuku station, or next to Yamada Denki (LABI) on Yasukuni Dori*

Around the station (west side)

Hakone Soba Honjin (箱根そば本陣) - Classic train station soba, nice and simple. Other simple dishes like curry are also sometimes available. *Soba from 290 yen • 6:30am-11pm • Near ticket gates for Odakyu trains on west side of station*

4) Coco Ichiban Curry House (CoCo 壱番屋) - The true taste of Japanese curry, and officially the largest curry restaurant chain in the world. *Curry + rice from 500 yen • 24h • Just outside exit D3, from Shinjuku-Nishiguchi station on the Toei Oedo Line*

5) Matsuya (松屋) - Gyudon and burger eat-in and takeaway. *Gyudon bowls from 290 yen • 24h • Around the corner from the above Coco Ichiban*

6) Ootoya (大戸屋) - Various Japanese set meals. *Meals from 750 yen • 11am-midnight • Opposite from above Coco Ichiban restaurant*

7) Oedo Sushi (回転寿司 大江戸) - Reliable conveyor belt sushi joint. *Sushi plates from 140 yen • 11am-11pm • Next to the above Ootoya*

North-west of the station

Take exit D5 of Shinjuku-Nishiguchi station, or walk from Shinjuku station. The following are in the order you'll see them:

8) Mos Burger (モス) - Mid-range burger chain, for those that need a western food fix with some Japanese twists, like 'rice burgers'. *Burgers from 220 yen • 5am-3am*

9) Sukiya (すき家) - Curry and gyudon eat-in and takeaway. *Meals from 360 yen • 24h*

10) Burger King (バーガーキング) - Cheaper burgers than Mos Burger, and a few odd Japan-only burgers. Occasionally has all-you-can eat whopper deals! *Burgers from 150 yen • 7am-11pm*

Shinjuku Dori (Street)

There are not so many budget options heading east down Shinjuku Dori from Shinjuku station, but it's still a supremely cool street to check out.

11) Shakey's (シェーキーズ) - All-you-can-eat pizza restaurant, with Japanese and seasonal themed flavors. Expect to be surprised by this imaginative menu! *Lunch time: adults 1160 yen, teens 880 yen, under junior high school age 500 yen. Dinner time: 1650 yen, 1000 yen, 500 yen • 11am-10:15pm • On right side, just before Isetan Department Store*

12) Sweets Paradise (スイーツパラダイス) - Stuff yourself at this all-you-can-eat sweets and cakes buffet. *Adults from 1080 yen, children from 860 yen • 11am-10pm • Shinjuku station, east exit (near Bic Camera)*

Nightlife

Piss Alley / Omoide Yokocho (思い出横丁)

Super cramped bar and counter restaurant area, this place requires a photo or two for being such an authentic Japanese night out spot. Prices have been increased to catch out tourists at some bars, so be careful if you want to eat or drink here. *Head out of Shinjuku west exit and then down to the right, or go out of exit D3 near Coco Ichiban restaurant (bar area is around and behind here)*

Golden Gai (新宿ゴールデン街)

A maze of more than 100 tiny bars to explore. Staff are often chatty and will offer great travel advice. Many of the bars have a cover charge, so look at the board outside or ask inside. Still really worth a walk around if you are not going in though, just to see how crammed in all the bars are. *Head east down Yasukuni Dori until you get to Mister Donut on the left after five to 10 minutes. Walk down the spiraling path*

Water bottle refill spots

The Tokyo Metropolitan Government Office and Shinjuku Gyoen have water fountains, plus Isetan Department store has a water cup machine on the stairs up from the 1st floor.

Shopping

East side

Yamada Denki LABI

Modern electronics megastore, with tax-free and electronics for use abroad. There is also a quieter branch on the west side. *10am-11:30 pm • From Shinjuku station, east exit, head north along the tracks, it's on the right on Yasukuni Dori*

Don Quijote (ドン・キホーテ)

Chaotic megastore full of any item you could imagine, from cheap souvenirs to fancy dress costumes to travel goods. This store is maybe the premier 'what the hell is going on?' Don Quijote experience. Great prices and tax-free options available. *24h • Opposite Yamada Denki LABI on Yasukuni Dori*

Bicqlo (ビックロ)

Bic Camera (huge electronics store with tax-free shopping) + Uniqlo (huge budget clothes store with tax-free shopping) = a budget traveler heaven! Also has GU, Uniqlo's new budget shop brand. *10am-10pm • East down Shinjuku Dori, not far from station*

LAOX Duty Free (ラオックス)

Mainly aimed at Chinese and Korean tourists looking to buy tax-free bags, jewelry and perfume. Worth having a quick look inside to see if a bargain can be had. *9am-9pm • Across the road from Isetan*

Tokyu Hands (東急ハンズ)

Tokyu Hands has everything from stationery to DIY goods to funny souvenirs and drinks. A bit more upmarket than Don Quijote, but prices can still be reasonable if doing tax-free shopping and looking out for special offers. *10am-9pm • Connected to Takashimaya department store*

ABC Mart (ABC マート)

Cheap shoe shop chain, with everything from sneakers to business shoes. *11am-10pm • Down Shinjuku Dori, just before Bicqlo*

Free sample hotspots

Isetan Department Store on Shinjuku Dori and Takashimaya have massive food courts in their basement floors. While the average item is quite pricey, there are plenty of free samples to be had, and it's also a fascinating window shopping experience. Just keep an eye out and don't make it look too obvious if you're not going to buy anything! Also be sure to share your pictures on Twitter, Facebook or Instagram and mention @SuperCheapJapan to show the world the amazing food on offer!

100-yen shops

Silk (シルク) - Near Yodobashi Camera on the east side. *10am-11pm*
Seria (セリア) - Inside Marui Annex on Shinjuku Dori. *11am-9pm*

Pharmacy (ドラッグ ストア)

Matsumoto Kiyoshi (マツモトキヨシ) has a shop opposite Bicuro (9am-10:30pm), while on the west side the best is Daikoku Drug (ダイコク ドラッグ), near Yamada Denki (8am-midnight).

How to get there and away

Shinjuku is on the circular Yamanote Line, Toei Oedo Line, Metro Marunouchi Line or Metro Shinjuku Line. From Tokyo station, take the Chuo Line to Shinjuku station (14 mins, 194 yen). From Shibuya station, take the Saikyo Line to Shinjuku station (6 mins, 154 yen). *Recommended rail passes: Tokyo Subway Ticket, Tokyo Metro 24-hour Ticket, Tokyo Metropolitan District Pass*

Tourist information (観光案内所)

A large tourist information center is found on the 1st floor of the Tokyo Metropolitan Building. It has excellent, free maps for hiking (9:30am-6:30pm). Shinjuku Bus Terminal also has one (6:30am-11pm).

Harajuku (原宿)

Takeshita Dori, Harajuku

Located between Shinjuku and Shibuya, Harajuku is the heartland of youth fashion and entertainment in Tokyo. It will provide plenty of splendid culture shock for a visitor, young or old. Many have heard the name Harajuku before, in popular culture or Japanese restaurant names, but it must really be seen to be believed. The area is full of independent boutiques and cafes, high-class shops and an increasing number of international chains, attracted by the status that being in Harajuku gives a brand.

Walk it and save!

To see the real Harajuku, you can't just visit Takeshita Dori and Omotesando. There are some fascinating back streets and more chilled out areas seconds away. It's the best way to see what Japan's young (and young at heart) are up to. Use the walking route on the map to take you to all the highlights in Harajuku.

Things to do

Meiji Jingu

Meiji Jingu Shrine (明治神宮)

Located next to Yoyogi Park, Meiji Jingu is Tokyo's biggest and busiest Shinto shrine. Dedicated to the souls of Emperor Meiji and his consort Empress Shoken, the shrine is surrounded by a large forest, which contains more than 100,000 trees from all over Japan and overseas. The crowds do flock here, but the wide open paths and calm environment keep this place tranquil and peaceful. While one section of the forest requires a fee, it is completely free to visit the rest of it. Traditional Japanese weddings often take place in the shrine in the afternoon, so you may strike lucky. If you do, be sure to post a picture on Facebook, Instagram or Twitter and mention @SuperCheapJapan! *FREE • Open at sunrise, closes at sundown (4-5pm) • Walk from Harajuku station, via wide bridge outside the main exit*

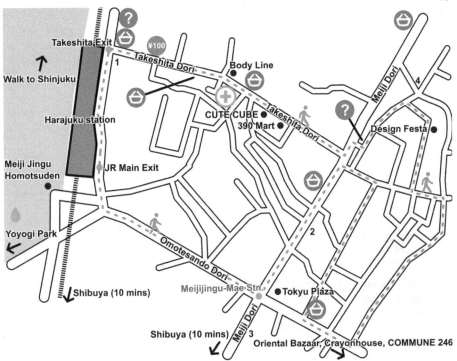

Homotsuden (Treasure Museum) (宝物殿)

Meiji Jingu has two treasure museums, for one entry fee. While it's not very popular with foreign tourists, the museums are an interesting insight into Japan's often forgotten history and its national treasures. Recent highlights include a 120 year old horse carriage used by a former emperor. *500 yen for both sites • 9am-4pm (note main building under reconstruction, check* http://www.meijijingu.or.jp/english/homotsuden/1.html *before going) • Main building in north of park*

Takeshita Dori (竹下通)

A wonderful street filled with a variety of colorful and crazy fashions. Along the way you will see people shouting out special deals, offering discounts on everything from watches to shoes to bags. Even with all the cheap deals, this is not the main reason to come here. The street is full of very cute, very colorful Japanese shops that amaze even the most hardened tourists. The following highlights are in order as you approach from Harajuku station.

Daiso (ダイソー)

A big 100-yen discount store. Get your drinks, cheap souvenirs and snacks here. *10am-9pm*

Bodyline

A treasure trove for anyone into cosplay or Lolita fashion, and an interesting peek into modern Japanese youth culture for others. Bodyline has prices starting from 200 yen for cute tights and decent boots can often be bought from around 3000 yen. Having said that, when there are clearance sales, shoes and tops can go from as low as 500 yen! *11am-8pm*

Cute Cube Harajuku

Small shopping mall full of unbelievably cute shops, such as a shop for Hello Kitty goods and the adorable cafe with character-themed meals. Also has a branch of Chicago, for reasonably priced vintage clothes. *10am-8pm*

390 Mart (Thank You Mart)

If you say three, then nine in Japanese, the sound is "Sankyuu", similar to the English word "Thank you". As you may have guessed, everything here is only 390 yen. Kawaii (cute) socks, t-shirts, denim jeans and hats, plus a good selection of tote bags are available. *11am-8pm*

Yoyogi Park (代々木公園)

A nice open park, great for playing games and sunbathing. Also one of Tokyo's most popular cherry blossom viewing areas. Come on Sunday for the Elvis dancers at the entrance! Cultural events and markets often take place here on the weekends in the summer, at the Yoyogi Outdoor Stage (代々木公園野外ステージ), just past the Yoyogi National Stadium. They usually have lots of stalls selling cheap Japanese food, as well as themed events, such as flea markets and food festivals. *FREE • 5am-8pm (until 5pm from mid Oct - Apr) • On the other side of Harajuku station*

Omotesando (表参道)

While this street is well known to tourists, apart from a few exceptions it is definitely not a place for budget travelers to go shopping. Think more Burberry and Louis Vuitton than 100-yen discount stores. It is still worth a walk up though, as there are interesting shopping streets that head off from Omotesando and a few shops for foreign tourists:

Tokyu Plaza Omotesando Harajuku (東急プラザ)

New shopping mall, with a spectacular entrance of huge metallic mirrors. It says its aim is to become a fashion theme park, and Tokyu Plaza certainly does a good job of spicing up shopping with a bunch of quirky shops. Grab a drink somewhere cheaper and chill out on the top, a super trendy rooftop garden looking over Harajuku. *10am-9pm • On left hand side after first main junction • http://omohara.tokyu-plaza.com/en/*

Kiddy Land (キデイランド)

Huge selection of toys for sale, from both Japanese and western companies. Really good fun for all ages. Get some tax-free toys for your kids, yourself or those back home for that magic 8% off. *11am-9pm • Down Omotesando from Tokyu Place, on right ride*

Oriental Bazaar (オリエンタルバザー)

One of the best souvenir shops in Japan. They have reasonably priced yukatas (traditional Japanese gowns) for sale and about any kind of gift you could want to take back. Staff are also very useful if you don't understand how things work or what their purpose is. *10am-7pm • Continue down Omotesando, a minute after first junction, on right • http://www.orientalbazaar.co.jp/*

Design Festa Gallery (デザインフェスタギャラリー)

A host of small galleries, more than 70 when at full capacity, showing off the latest up-and-coming artists. All sorts of styles, and ever changing exhibitions on display. Design Festa has become a bit of an institution in Harajuku, and makes going to an expensive gallery unnecessary for most. *FREE • Times vary by gallery • After walking down Takeshita Dori from Harajuku station, cross the road and continue forward. Take the second left, it's on the right side • http://www.designfestagallery.com/index_en.html*

COMMUNE 246

A super hip community space opened in 2014, COMMUNE 246 is a micro-village with lots to do. As well as cool workspaces and coffee spots for local workers, there are also a host of food trucks selling decent meals and snacks. Menus are often imaginative and not too pricey. *11am-10pm • Head down Omotesando Dori to Omotesando station, then head to the left at the junction. COMMUNE 246 is on the right, one-minute down • http://commune2nd.com/*

Budget food

It's a bit difficult to find cheap food in Harajuku, so definitely stick with the cheap chain restaurants and convenience stores, or see what is on offer in Yoyogi Park.

Budget restaurants on map

1) Yoshinoya (吉野家) - Gyudon and curry. *Bowls from 330 yen • 5am-2pm*
2) Tempura Tenya (天丼てんや) - Deep-fried fish and vegetables. *Bowls from 500 yen • 11am-11pm*

Local budget food

3) Ichiran Ramen (一蘭) - Ramen bar that focuses on Tonkotsu (pork) based ramen, and does it pretty damned well. *Ramen from 790 yen • 10am-10:45pm • Walk down Omotesando from Harajuku station, then take a right at first junction and look for 一蘭 characters on other side (opposite Metro exit 7)*
4) Nagaraya Bento (ながらや) - Pick up a posher than usual bento at this local shop. *Bento boxes from 680 yen • 10am-5pm • Cross road at end of Takeshita Dori (if coming from Harajuku station), walk down narrow street on left for 2 mins*
5) Crayonhouse (クレヨンハウス) – All-you-can eat restaurant with lots of great options for kids and a mostly organic menu. Gets very busy, so arrive early. *Lunch: Adults 1296 yen, children 648 yen. Dinner: Adults 2160 yen, children 1080 yen, under 6 years 756 yen • 11am-11pm • Head down Omotesando Dori, then a little down the street between Hugo Boss and Coach (opposite the Apple store)*

Cheap supermarkets (スーパー)

There are no supermarkets, but plenty of large convenience stores around.

Water bottle refill spots

There are some water fountains in Yoyogi Park, but it could be quite a trek just to refill your bottle. Head to Daiso for cheap drinks and snacks.

Pharmacy (ドラッグストア)

Matsukiyo (薬 マツモトキヨシ) has a pharmacy down Takeshita Dori (9:30am - 10pm).

How to get there and away

By rail

From Shinjuku station, take the JR Yamanote Line to Harajuku station (4 mins, 133 yen). From Tokyo station, take the JR Yamanote Line to Harajuku station (26 mins, 194 yen). If using the Metro, head to Meiji-jingumae station on the **Fukutoshin** or **Chiyoda** lines. *Recommended rail passes: Tokyo Subway Ticket, Tokyo Metro 24-hour Ticket, Tokyo Metropolitan District Pass*

Walk it and save!

To/from Shinjuku, we have walked the distance in under 30 minutes. The best route is to go via the grounds of Meiji Jingu, which has an entrance at the south near Harajuku station and another in the north near Shinjuku station. Most visitors will go around these grounds anyway, so it's a worthwhile money saving idea. Just stay on the west side of the JR Yamanote Line tracks (look out for the trains with light green lines on them) and you will get to your destination.

Tourist information (観光案内所)

H.I.S has an unofficial, but still very helpful tourist information center (10am-5:30pm), a little further north from the entrance to Takeshita Dori if coming from Harajuku station. There is an official one, called Moshi Moshi Box, down Takeshita Dori (10am-6pm).

Shibuya (渋谷)

One of Tokyo's most lively and colorful neighborhoods, Shibuya is most famous as a youth fashion hotspot and the busiest road crossing you will ever see. Originally the site of a castle belonging to the Shibuya clan, since the introduction of the Yamanote Line it has become one of the main clubbing, shopping and entertainment areas in Tokyo.

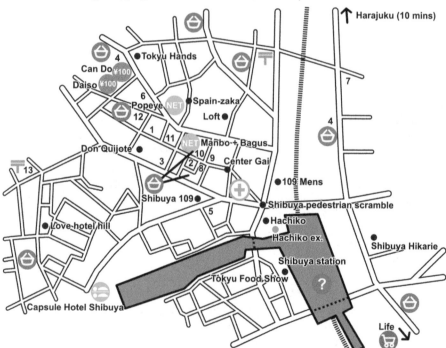

The station is a real maze, so use the locations on the map (e.g. Hachiko or Shibuya Hikarie) with the boards inside the station that direct visitors to the corresponding exits.

Things to do

Free activities near station

Shibuya pedestrian scramble (スクランブル交差点)
Every few minutes thousands of people walk over the world's most famous road crossing. Make sure you bring a camera! Best spot is on the second floor of Starbucks. *Hachiko exit*

Hachiko statue (ハチ公)
The famous statue and meeting point in Shibuya. After his owner died, a dog called Hachiko came to the station every day to meet his owner. The dog became famous and this statue was made in dedication to him. A cute cat has also made the statue its home, so be sure to take a photo of Shibuya's most iconic spot. *Hachiko exit*

Love hotel hill (ラブホテル坂)
Shibuya is an expensive place to live, so many people still live with their family. Many therefore head over to this prized love hotel area for a bit of privacy with their partner. This area is full of these hotels offering rooms for very cheap prices. Even if you are not staying, it's definitely worth a walk around to see all the cheesy architecture and bright lights. *All night!* • *Take a left after Don Quijote and walk up*

Free sample heavens

Tokyu Food Show (東急フードショー)
A treasure chest of Japanese food, plus international stalls to spice things up. With countless stalls, you can spend lots of time just wandering around, trying out free samples as you go. *10am-9pm • Basement of Tokyu Department Store, west side of station*

Shibuya Hikarie (渋谷ヒカリエ)
A fancy department store with modern shops, restaurants and a nice food area downstairs. Has even more stalls handing out free samples than Tokyu Food Show, so try lots and see what you like. *10am-9pm • Exit 15 / east exit*

Center Gai (渋谷センター街)
Shibuya's main shopping street, also known as Basketball Street. Center Gai is full of game arcades, fast food restaurants, fashion boutiques and bars. The food options are excellent and the area comes to life in the evening, with plenty of raucous businessmen and teenagers. *Across the Shibuya pedestrian scramble*

Shopping around Shibuya station

Shibuya 109
Worth a walk around to see what is hot and what is not in the world of youth fashion in Japan. 109 is the place to be for upcoming brands, and regarded as a stamp of quality for them. Staff are very friendly and will help you out if you don't know what things are! *10am-9pm • Exit 3A*

Tokyu Hands (東急ハンズ)
Full of crazy, strange Japanese goods for you to laugh at and enjoy. Back scratchers, weird massage chairs, crazy robot toys and some unimaginable goods. Great for souvenirs and any novelties you want to take home. *10am-9pm • 5 minutes down Inokashira Dori*

Mega Don Quijote (ドン・キホーテ)
Cheaper prices than Tokyu Hands, this megastore has everything from second-hand jewelry to clothes, to cheap snacks. *24h • Exit 3A, then down the road, on the right*

100-yen shops

Can Do (キャンドゥ) - Opposite Tokyu Hands. *10am-10pm*
Daiso (ダイソー) - Another great 100-yen shop nearby. *10am-9pm*

Pharmacy (ドラッグストア)

Matsumoto Kiyoshi (マツモトキヨシ) is on the way to 109 (24h).

Budget food

Budget chain restaurants on map

1) Tenka Ippin (天下一品) - Ramen. *Ramen from 700 yen • 11am-3am*
2) Matsuya (松屋) - Rice bowls and curry. *Gyudon bowls from 290 yen • 24h*
3) Ootoya (大戸屋) - Japanese set meals. *Sets from 750 yen • 11am-11pm*
4) Hidakaya (日高屋) - Ramen and gyoza dumplings. *Ramen from 390 yen • 10:30am-3:30pm*
5) Yoshinoya (吉野家) - Gyudon and curry. *Bowls from 330 yen • 24h*
6) Sukiya (すき家) - Gyudon and curry. *Bowls from 360 yen • 24h*
7) Tempura Tenya (天丼てんや) – Tempura. *Bowls from 500 yen • 11am-11pm*
8) Wendy's First Kitchen (ファーストキッチン) - Cheap soups, burgers and pasta. *Pasta from 580 yen, burgers from 370 yen • 5am-1am*

Local budget food

Best spots along Center Gai, in order from the station.
9) Yanbaru Okinawa Soba (やんばる 沖縄そば) - Set dishes and soba from Okinawa. *Noodles from 650 yen • 11am-11:30pm*
10) Yaro Ramen (野郎ラーメン) - Large sized ramen. *Ramen from 500 yen • 24h*
11) Kamukura Ramen (どうとんぼり神座) - Big menu, with English explanations on how to eat it and vegetarian options. *Ramen from 680 yen • 9am-8am*
12) Shakey's Pizza (シェーキーズ) - All-you-can-eat pizza restaurant, with Japanese and seasonal themed flavors. *Lunch time: adults 930 yen, teens 600 yen, under junior high school age 380 yen. Dinner time: 1540 yen, 1030 yen, 510 yen • 11am-11pm*
13) Okonomiyaki Mura (お好み焼 むら) - All-you-can-eat Japanese pancakes, called Okonomiyaki. *90 mins for 1980 yen or Okonomiyaki from 780 yen • 12pm-3am*

Cheap supermarkets (スーパー)

Life Supermarket (ライフ渋谷東店) is a 10/15-minute walk away from Shibuya station on Meiji Dori, to the south and along the narrow river (9am-1am).

How to get there and away

From Shinjuku station, take the JR Yamanote Line to Shibuya station (6 mins, 154 yen). From Tokyo station, take the JR Yamanote Line to Shibuya station (24 mins, 194 yen). Also on Tokyo Metro **Fukutoshin**, **Hanzomon** and Ginza lines. *Recommended rail passes: Tokyo Subway Ticket, Tokyo Metro 24-hour Ticket, Tokyo Metropolitan District Pass*

Tourist information (観光案内所)

Just outside the Hachiko exit, inside the adorable old green train carriage (9am-6pm).

Meguro and Ebisu (目黒と恵比寿)

Well known to expats and fashionable Japanese, Meguro and Ebisu are not tourist hotspots, but places that everyday people love to hang out at. While 20-somethings go to Shibuya or Harajuku, these areas cater to more sophisticated and quieter tastes. Some restaurants and bars can therefore be a bit expensive, but if you follow the tips below you will be able to enjoy a budget day away from the crowds.

Things to do

Meguro Parasitological Museum (目黒寄生虫館)
The Meguro Parasitological Museum is a truly 'only in Japan' experience! This museum is dedicated to bugs, parasites and other creepy crawlies. It claims to be the only such museum in the world, and the experience is definitely not a standard touristy one. Be prepared to be both shocked and amazed! Especially at the nine meter long tape-worm taken from one rather unfortunate victim. *FREE • 10am-5pm (closed Mondays and Tuesdays or the following day if these are national holidays) • From Meguro station, head west along Meguro Dori, crossing over a large bridge. Walk up until you get to a Royal Host restaurant on your right. The museum is a little further on, across the road*

Institute for Nature Study, National Museum of Nature and Science (国立科学博物館附属自然教育園)
Need to get back into nature, and quick? This surprisingly unknown forest in the heart of Tokyo is a great spot for an easy woodland walk or a spot of bird watching. A true sanctuary for natural beauty and birdlife, the mixed forest is easy to navigate. *310 yen • 9am-5pm (closed Mondays) • 10-minute walk along Meguro Dori from the east exit of JR Meguro station*

Naka-Meguro (中目黒)
While this area has a reputation for being expensive and upper-class, Meguro River (目黒川) is a cool place to chill out in the evening with a drink or two. There are convenience stores around if you want to buy cheap beer or a bento to save on cash. Naka-Meguro is particularly popular during the cherry blossom season, when the river is lined with sakura trees. *Naka-Meguro station or 10-minute walk down main road from Ebisu, heading west*

Museum of Yebisu Beer (ヱビスビール記念館)
Mainly known as Ebisu Beer, one of the top three beer brands in Japan. The museum features a good number of displays on the history of Yebisu Beer, as well as Japanese beer in general. The Tasting Salon (reasonable fees apply) is the highlight here, and the shop features everything from branded beer jugs to beer jelly. *FREE • 11am-7pm (closed Mondays and New Year holidays) • Once at Ebisu station follow the signs to the museum (5 minutes on foot)*

Budget food

Around the stations are the usual budget chains, but most of the spots of interest are away from the stations, so consider eating before visiting these.

Cheap supermarkets (スーパー)
There is a Seijo Ichi supermarket inside Ebisu station, which can be a little pricey (9am-11pm). Tokyu Store, just outside Meguro station's west exit is better (10am-11pm).

100-yen shops
Can Do (キャンドゥ) - Inside the Tokyu Store building. *10am-10pm*

How to get there and away

Meguro

On the JR Yamanote Line, Metro Namboku Line and Toei Mita Line. From Shibuya, take the JR Yamanote Line to Meguro station (154 yen, 5 mins).

Ebisu

One more stop on the JR Yamanote Line from Meguro. Also on JR Shonan-Shinjuku Line, JR Saikyo Line and Metro Hibiya Line. *Recommended rail passes: Tokyo Subway Ticket, Tokyo Metro 24-hour Ticket, Tokyo Metropolitan District Pass*

Shin-Okubo (新大久保)

Idol heaven on the streets of Koreatown

Sometimes known as Koreatown, the Shin-Okubo area is the place to see how the cute and crazy aspects of these two countries combine. It's full of idol shops selling posters, CDs and DVDs of the latest stars, as well as the heartthrobs of the past. It attracts both the young and old, who come here to immerse themselves in Korean culture, fashion and cosmetics.

Walk it and save

The best way to enjoy Shin-Okubo is to walk it. Head out of the north exit of Shin-Okubo or Okubo station and head right (to the east). Head down the main street, popping down any side streets of interest. Around the point that you get to Can Do 100-yen shop, cross the road and loop back. The side streets often have more novel and cheaper shops to explore.

Budget food

There are many cheap takeout spots in Shin-Okubo, as well as some reasonably priced all-you-can-eat restaurants, most of which have English menus. If you want to stuff yourself on all-you-can-eat Korean BBQ, look out for the tabehodai (食べ放題) signs, with a good price being between 1500-2000 yen per person. They are littered along the main street, as well as down the side roads. As for cheap stacks, there are plenty of stalls selling favorites such as Korean hotdogs (ハッドグ) for 300-400 yen and Tteok-bokki (トッポッキ), stir-fried rice cakes, for around 300-500 yen. It's best to have a stroll and see what grabs your interest the most!

Cheap supermarkets (スーパー)
No-frills Kobebussan (業務スーパー) is between Shin-Okubo and Okubo stations (9am-9pm).

Shopping

100-yen shops
Can Do (キャンドゥ) – Lots of great options for foreign travelers. *10am-10pm • 10 minutes down the street from Shin-Okubo station, on the right*

Pharmacy (ドラッグストア)
In addition to the countless Korean stores selling Korean cosmetics, there is a Matsumoto pharmacy (マツモトキヨシ) outside Shin-Okubo station selling more standard items (24h).

How to get there and away

From Shinjuku, take the JR Yamanote Line to Shin-Okubo (3 mins, 133 yen). Nearby Okubo is on the JR Sobu Line. It's also possible to walk to Shin-Okubo from Shinjuku, just head north for 15 minutes. *Recommended rail pass: Tokyo Metropolitan District Pass*

Shimo-Kitazawa (下北沢)

Shimo-Kitazawa is a trendy district with plenty of second-hand shops, bars, record shops, interesting fashions and nice cafes and restaurants. If you are into buying cheap clothes, CDs or ornaments, Shimo-Kitazawa is a must. While tourists tend to flock to the main areas of Shibuya and Shinjuku, 'Shimo' is where residents go to hang out and do a bit of budget shopping. It's where all the cool, young people go!

Shopping and other things to do

The best way to experience Shimo-Kitazawa is to walk around randomly and just soak it in. The streets are so narrow and numerous, so don't worry too much about getting lost. Just enjoy walking down any street that looks interesting and you should come across some nice spots. There are too many discount, thrift and second-hand stores to list them all, so here are some highlights. There are many more between these and down nearby side streets.

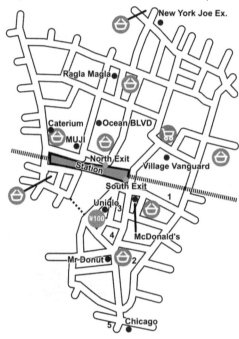

Ocean BLVD (古著屋 Ocean BLVD)

More than a dozen small shops selling cheap clothes, souvenirs, ornaments, retro toys and much more. The tightly packed-in shops are all independent ones, which gives the place a slightly chaotic but fun atmosphere. *11am-8pm*

Ragla Magla (ラグラマグラ)

All clothing items and accessories are 990 yen at this shore, from blouses to bags to coats. They also have further occasional deals, such as the completely nuts 2980 yen 'all you can pack in your shopping basket' sale. *12am-9pm*

New York Joe Exchange

Located in a former public bathhouse, this store has a good selection of very cheap, but good quality clothing from a variety of brands. The staff are also very knowledgeable about current fashions and are super helpful. First Sunday of every month also has a 50% off everything sale. *12am-8pm • Continue down the road from Ocean BLVD, take right at Lawson convenience store. It's on the left side*

Village Vanguard (ヴィレッジヴァンガード)

Large branch of the crazy pack-em-in variety store. This one is great for funny souvenirs, full of 'only in Japan' items as well as books and amusing costumes. Worth a visit even if you have absolutely no money to spend on shopping. *10am-midnight*

Chicago (シカゴ)

The largest branch in Tokyo of this used clothing store. Chicago has a load of reasonably priced clothing, from international brands to local vintage ones. They also have a large selection of used kimonos, yukatas, obi (traditional belts), Japanese slippers and accessories. *11am-8pm*

Caterium (キャットカフェ キャテリアム)

Chilled out cafe, with the difference being all the cats walking about! Visitors can dress up the cats in all sorts of cute clothing, or have a play using plenty of adorable toys. They have also started all-you-can-eat shaved ice for 200 yen! *1 hour 1000 yen (includes one drink) • 11am-9pm • From the north exit, head left and up past Muji. Take a right, and Caterium is just above 7-Eleven*

Uniqlo (ユニクロ)

A quieter branch of Japan's most popular cheap clothes shop chain. *10am-9pm*

100-yen shops

Daiso (ダイソー) - in the small shopping mall of the above Uniqlo. *10am-9pm*

Getting around

You will get lost here, at least once, but don't worry as it's part of the charm of Shimo-Kitazawa. If you get lost, use the map and try to retrace your steps using the various landmarks. If all is lost, head back to the station ("eki" in Japanese) and walk around it until you get to your desired station exit. It's all very walkable.

Budget food

Apart from some chain restaurants, there are other cheap options available for food in Shimo-Kitazawa, but most budget travelers should head to Ozeki supermarket.

1) CONA - Delicious 'one coin' pizzas, but in a stylish, laidback setting. Note that after 5pm there is a 300 yen cover charge, so come at lunch. *Pizzas from 500 yen • 12am-11pm*

2) Hiroki - Hiroshima style okonomiyaki (Japanese pancake) restaurant, possibly the best in Tokyo. This style has soba or udon inside the okonomiyaki. *Okonomiyaki from 900 yen • 12am-9:45pm • Continue down from CONA, head right at the first intersection, then walk a minute down*

3) Matsuya (松屋) - Gyudon and burger eat-in and takeaway. *Meals from 290 yen • 24h*

4) Hidakaya (日高屋) - Tokyo's super cheap ramen shop. There are also slightly more expensive, but more authentic ramen joints on the same street. *Ramen from 390 yen • 24h*

5) Ohsho (餃子の王将) - Chinese inspired ramen, fried rice and gyoza dumpling chain with a large, English menu. *Ramen from 500 yen, dumplings from 240 yen • 11:30am-4am*

Cheap supermarkets (スーパー)

Ozeki (オオゼキ) is a particularly good supermarket for cheap sushi. Also has a variety of cheap bento boxes, snacks and drinks (9:30am-6pm).

Pharmacy (ドラッグストア)

There are several around the station. An easy one to get to is Ippondo Drug Store (ドラッグストア 一本堂), near Vanguard (10am-10pm).

How to get there and away

From Shinjuku, take the Odakyu Line to Shimo-Kitazawa station (7 mins, 150 yen). From Shibuya, take the Keio Inokashira Line to Shimo-Kitazawa (6 mins, 124 yen).

Koenji (高円寺)

Koenji, like Shimo-Kitazawa, is a trendy town with many cheap shops, cafes, bars and restaurants. Known as Tokyo's main counter-culture area, it features some great second-hand book and music shops. A great place to escape the tourist crowds of Shinjuku and Shibuya, Koenji is often a favorite spot for foreigners living, rather than just traveling, in Tokyo.

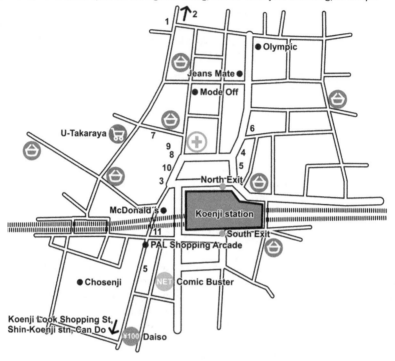

Things to do

The best way to experience Koenji is to walk around the station, up the various shopping streets, looking for some bargains. Koenji is really a great place for a spot of window shopping, and purchasing a few interesting goods. The counter-culture vibe has also helped to develop some great independent, but not too pricey, restaurants and take-out shops.

Chosenji Temple (長仙寺)

Not essential, as this is a rather small and not so impressive temple, but if you want a quick break from walking around it does make for a relaxing spot. *FREE • 24h • Head right after St. Marc Cafe down PAL Shopping Arcade (高円寺パル商店街)*

Shopping

Looking for cheap clothes? Second-hand or recycled goods? Cute but stylish accessories or ornaments? Koenji is going to blow your socks off if you are into these things. Countless independent shops sell all sorts of goods, so give yourself at least an hour or two to explore.

South of Koenji station

PAL Shopping Arcade (高円寺パル商店街)
An interesting spot for a bit of shopping, PAL has more chains than elsewhere, but still has a few gems. Village Vanguard (ヴィレッジヴァンガード) is an iconic, crazy shop full of random 'only in Japan' items, magazines and posters to take home (10am-midnight) and the game arcade has plenty of 100-yen games to play. *Take the south exit from Koenji station, then take a right turn and walk a little until you see the PAL sign above*

Koenji Look Shopping Street (高円寺ルック商店街)
Lined with second-hand and antique stores, plus some funky cafes and tiny up-and-coming restaurants. Prices may be higher than the 100-yen shops, but there are some real bargains to be found. If buying lots, don't be afraid to haggle, even though this is Japan! *Continue on from PAL Shopping Arcade or start at Shin-Koenji (Metro Marunouchi Line) and walk up*

North of Koenji station

Olympic (オリンピック)
Cheap bicycles, everyday essentials and basic fashion items at not too bad a price. *10am-9pm • Once out of Koenji station (north exit), head down the road with the orange Yoshinoya restaurant*

Jeans Mate (ジーンズメイト)
Yes, the information below is correct, this is a 24-hour jean shop. Cheap T-shirts, shoes and of course jeans, plus tax-free available for foreign tourists (remember your passport). *24h • Opposite Olympic*

Mode Off (モードオフ)
Second-hand and retro clothes, bags, hats and accessories available in this large store. *11am-9pm • Head out of Koenji station (north exit), then up the street with the Sundrug*

100-yen shops
Daiso (ダイソー) - A little small, but has all the 100-yen essentials. *10am-9pm*
Can Do (キャンドゥ) - Much larger choice than Daiso, with a good selection on everyday essentials. *10am-9pm • All the way down Koenji Look Shopping Street*

Pharmacy (ドラッグストア)
Sundrug (サンドラッグ高円寺店) is across from Koenji station, north exit (10am-10:45pm).

Budget food

1) Sempre Pizza (センプレ ピッツァ) - We don't know how this place keeps things so cheap, but they sell real Italian pizzas for only a few coins. *Pizzas from 380 yen • 11:30am-10pm • Head out of Koenji station (north exit), head up the street with the Sundrug (サンドラッグ高円寺店), take a left at the end and walk down*

2) Floresta Nature Doughnuts (フロレスタ) - Fancy doughnuts and some good choices for those who want a healthier, organic sweet snack. *Doughnuts from 150 yen • 9am-9pm • From Sempre Pizza, take a right turn and walk up the street*

3) Mister Donut (ミスタードーナツ) - Cheaper option for doughnuts, with a huge choice. Also sells cheap snacks like sausage rolls, soups and breads. *Doughnuts from 100 yen, breads from 120 yen • 7am-11pm • Near McDonald's at Koenji station, north exit*

4) Yoshinoya (吉野家) - Gyudon eat-in and takeaway. *Meals from 330 yen • 24h • North exit of Koenji station*

5) Kaiten Misakiko (海鮮三崎港) - Some of the cheapest sushi in Tokyo, and great quality. *Sushi plate from 110 yen + tax • 11am-11pm • One branch is outside Koenji station (north exit), on the right next to Yoshinoya. The other is a minute down PAL Shopping Arcade*

6) Hotto Motto (ほっともっと) - Good bento spot in Koenji, with a varied menu. *Bento boxes from 390 yen • 8am-11pm • From Koenji station (north exit), walk a little past Yoshinoya on the right. Hotto Motto is on the right side*

7) Mos Burger (モス) - Get your western food fix with some Japanese twists, like 'rice burgers' and more. *Burgers from 220 yen • 8am-11pm*

8) Matsuya (松屋) - Gyudon and burger eat-in and takeaway. *Meals from 290 yen • 24h • On the left side after exiting Koenji station, north exit*

9) Bochi Bochi Okonomiyaki (ぼちぼち) - Reasonably priced okonomiyaki (Japanese pancake) restaurant. *Plates from 800 yen • 11am-11pm • Just above Matsuya*

10) Tenya Tempura (天丼てんや) - Cheap tempura bowls and plates. *Bowls from 500 yen • 11am-11:30pm • On the left side after exiting Koenji station, north exit*

11) Kyotaru Sushi (京樽) - Cheap sushi stall, with discounts in the evenings before closing. *Sushi boxes from 490 yen • 9am-10pm • Behind McDonald's, outside Koenji station, north exit*

Cheap supermarkets (スーパー)

U-Takaraya (ユータカラヤ) is near the north exit (10am-9am).

Nightlife

There are a host of cheap outside bars around the station, and under the tracks, especially on the left as you exit on the north side. We recommend having a walk around and seeing which one you like the look of. There are also some yakitori restaurants around here as well, but be careful with ordering, as the prices can go sky high if you get more than a few sticks.

Free wifi locations

Wifi reception is awful in Koenji station, so head to the McDonald's outside the station.

How to get there and away

From Shinjuku station, take the Chuo Line or Sobu Line to Koenji station (6 mins, 154 yen). From Tokyo station, take the Chuo Line to Koenji station (27 mins, 302 yen). You need to change at Nakano station on weekends. *Recommended rail passes: Tokyo Metropolitan District Pass, Tokyo Subway Ticket, Tokyo Metro 24-hour Ticket. If using a subway pass, go to Shin-koenji station on the Marunouchi Line, and walk north up Koenji Look Shopping Street (高円寺ルック商店街).*

Kichijoji (吉祥寺)

Kichijoji is a nice place to spend a cheap day, just walking around and doing an odd bit of shopping, eating or relaxing in the park. It's the most interesting suburban area outside central Tokyo, and has many things to keep all types of people occupied. Kichijoji is well worth spending an afternoon in with its blend of local bargains and less crowded tourist spots.

Walk it and save!

Kichijoji is all walkable on foot, another reason it's great for budget travelers. It can be a bit confusing to know where exactly you are, so use the landmarks on the map to help you out. Use the recommended walking route as well. When you get to the park, leave from the other exit, as shown in the map.

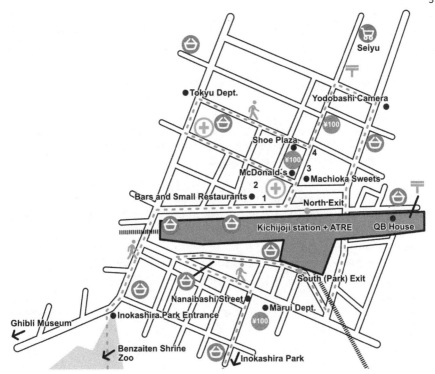

Things to do

Inokashira Park

Inokashira Park is a great place to come during the cherry blossom season or during the autumn colors. Other times, it is a relaxing spot for a stroll, especially on weekends with impromptu flea market stalls selling inventive goods and performers doing all kinds of free performances by the lake. *FREE • 24h • Short walk south of Kichijoji station*

Ghibli Museum (三鷹の森ジブリ美術館)

A house full of the same kind of magic that makes Ghibli films so great, the building looks like it was taken off a set of one of the movies. Original artwork, playrooms and a cinema showing short films, plus a special exhibition every year. Note that you cannot buy tickets on the day. Check the Ghibli Museum website for how to buy tickets or go to a Lawson convenience store to buy beforehand (ask the staff for help). *Ages 19 and over 1000 yen, Ages 13 to 18 700 yen, Ages 7 to 12 400 yen, Ages 4 to 6 100 yen • 10am-6pm • Well signposted from park •* http://www.ghibli-museum.jp/en/

Benzaiten Shrine (井の頭弁財天)

A beautiful shrine on a little island in the park. Benzaiten is a Japanese Buddhist goddess, based on the Hindu goddess Saraswati. The shrine therefore has a few touches from both religions. *FREE • 24h*

Inokashira Park Zoo (井の頭自然文化園)

A reasonably priced zoo with a good selection of animals and birds. Nothing too crazy in here, but if you like animals (and have children to entertain) it's worth it. *Adults 400 yen (FREE with Grutto Pass), Children (13-15) 150 yen, Children (12 and under) FREE • 9:30am-5pm (closed on Monday)*

North of Kichijoji station

There are all sorts of businesses here, such as cheap clothes shops, nice restaurants and occasional 'pop-up' food stalls.

Yodobashi Camera

A huge, huge electronics store, and without the crowds of Akihabara or Shinjuku. Tax-free shopping available. *9:30am-10pm • Up the wide road from the north exit*

Bars and small restaurants

Opposite the Baskin Robbins ice cream shop to the left of the north exit, be sure to explore this unique area. Most of the bars are a little expensive, but it has lots of atmosphere with its small narrow lanes packed with bars and restaurants.

Sun Road (吉祥寺サンロード商店街)

Great place to start your shopping and people watching in Kichijoji. Head out from the north exit of Kichijoji station. Sun Road is the roofed shopping arcade with the McDonald's. Also be sure to head off to the many interesting roads and side paths along it.

Machioka Sweets (おかしのまちおか)

A treasure trove of Japanese candy and soda drinks, this charming shop often has great deals to entice people in, like drinks for 60 yen or candy value multipacks. *10am-9pm*

100-yen shops

$1 drinks, gifts, snacks and more at Daiso (ダイソー) or CanDo (キャン・ドゥ). *10am-9pm*

Shoe Plaza (シュープラザ)

Bargain shoe superstore, one of many you will see around these shopping arcades. *10am-9pm*

QB House

1000 yen haircutters. Get yourself the cheapest haircut of your life (and quickest, at under 10 minutes), or have a peek in at the huge vacuums they use to quickly suck up the hair on the floor! *1000 yen per cut • 10am-9pm • Lower level of Atre, the shopping mall connected to the station*

Nanaibashi Street (七井橋通り)

A really cool shopping street with loads of trendy shops and fancy cafes, so worth checking out to see what daily life is like in Kichijoji. Not generally the best place to get any bargains, but you may come across a sale or two if you're lucky! *Head south from Kichijoji. Nanaibashi Street is down the side of Marui Department Store.*

West of Kichijoji

There are a few nice spots a short train ride away from Kichijoji station, both of which are accessible with the JR Tokyo Wide Pass:

Showa Kinen Park (昭和記念公園)

A former US air base converted to a large garden complex, Showa Kinen (Memorial) Park has so much to offer. The grand size allows for multiple different gardens, such as a Bonsai garden and cherry blossom areas, that change season to season. If you are stopping off here on the way to somewhere else you could just check the free area outside the entrance, otherwise it's worth giving yourself at least a few hours inside to explore all that is on offer. *Adults 450 yen, children FREE • 9:30am-5pm, until 6pm in summer (closed Mondays, or following day if Monday is a holiday) • From Kichijoji, take the Chuo Line to Tachikawa (19 mins, 216 yen), then it's a short walk*

Edo-Tokyo Open Air Museum (江戸東京たてもの園)

A fun outdoor museum featuring buildings from 17th to 20th century Edo (the old name for Tokyo). It has lots of in-depth history for adults, but the attractions are also enjoyable for the little ones. Highlights include an old bath house, grand mansions and an old-fashioned shopping street. *Adults 400 yen, children FREE • 9:30am-5:30pm (closed Mondays) • From Kichijoji, take the Chuo Line to Musashi-koganei (12mins, 165 yen), then take the Seibu bus from bus stop 2 or 3 to Koganei Park West Gate (10 mins, 180 yen extra). Alternatively, it's a 30 min walk north, up the main road*

Budget food

1) Fuji Soba (富士そば) - No frills soba and udon bar, with small curries and other side dishes. *Soba from 290 yen • 24h • Opposite Baskin Robbins, near the north exit*

2) Hamonika Quina (ハモニカ・クイナ) - Tacorice is a famous Okinawa invention, combining Japanese rice with a topping of what would be a filling to a Mexican taco. This one is the best in Tokyo. *Tacorice from 690 yen • 11:30am-10pm • In collection of small bars and restaurants opposite Baskin Robbins, from the north exit*

3) Shakey's (シェーキーズ) - All-you-can-eat pizza restaurant, with Japanese and seasonal themed flavors. Expect to be surprised by this imaginative menu! *Lunch time: adults 1160 yen, teens 880 yen, under junior high school age 500 yen. Dinner time: 1650 yen, 1000 yen, 500 yen • 11am-10:15pm • On Sun Road*

4) Matsuya (松屋) - Gyudon and burger eat-in and takeaway. *Meals from 290 yen • 24h • Half way down Sun Road*

Cheap supermarkets (スーパー)

Seiyu has a huge supermarket towards the end of Sun Road (10am-11pm).

Pharmacy (ドラッグ ストア)

Sundrug (サンドラッグ サンロード店) is on Sun Road (10am-10:15pm).

How to get there and away

From Shinjuku station, take the JR Chuo Line to Kichijoji station (216 yen, 15 mins). From other stations, first get to Shinjuku station. If using a Tokyo Metropolitan District Pass, you need to pay from Nishi-Ogikubo to Kichijoji (133 yen).

Nakano (中野)

Missed out by almost every tourist, Nakano is worth stopping off at for an hour or two if on the way to Koenji or Kichijoji. It's also known as a kind of Akihabara of the west side, so has some useful shops selling comic, figurines and other geeky delights. Nakano can get busy, but it feels like a much more down-to-earth location, as it's not really on many tourist maps.

Things to do

Nakano Sun Mall (中野サンモール)

Just head out of the north exit of Nakano station and walk straight ahead to this covered shopping arcade. The main attraction here is the food (see below), but there are also some shops selling discount shoes, watches and clothes.

Nakano Broadway (中野ブロードウェイ)

Right at the end of Sun Mall, this old-fashioned shopping mall is packed with manga, anime and game shops, as well as the odd maid café and gaming arcade. Even if you are not into such things, it's still a fascinating place to walk around and experience. Here are some highlights:

Mandarake
Several branches in the mall, each one focusing on a certain geeky interest. *12pm-8pm*

Junkworld

Sells and buys second-hand computer and electronic parts. *10am-9pm*

Art galleries

Often on the third or fourth floor, local artists show off their latest works. The work is usually very experimental, and often quite shocking!

Antique Ajisai

Shows off antique dolls and odd novelties from across the world. *11:30am-7pm*

Side streets

Take a right turn down one of the side streets as you go up Nakano Sun Mall and you will enter quite a treasure trove of food alleys and izakaya (Japanese pubs). While not so much geared towards budget consumers, it's an atmospheric place to see the locals and take some pictures.

Toshimaen Niwa no Yu (豊島園 庭の湯)

An excellent hot spring for beginners and addicts alike. It has a mixed section (bring your swimsuit!), as well as gender separated bathing sections, so it's a good place if you are a bit shy about entering a Japanese hot spring. There are a large variety of baths, from large lukewarm baths to hot 'one man' baths, as well as various saunas. Note that tattoos are not allowed. *2310 yen (1295 yen after 6pm) • 10am-11pm • Short walk from Toshimaen on the Toei Subway Oedo Line or with Seibu from Ikebukuro. If coming from Nakano, head to Ochiai on the Tozai Line, then make a short walk to Nakai station on the Oedo Line. From here you can proceed to Toshimaen station*

Budget food

Sun Mall is full of budget food joints, you are really spoilt for choice. Here are a few highlights, approaching from the station:

Refutei (おやき処 れふ亭) – Delicious custard filled sponge cakes. *From 150 yen • 11am-9pm • Just before entering Nakano Sun Mall, on the right*

Gindako (銀だこ) – Cheap takoyaki (octopus balls). *From 550 yen • 10am-11pm • Nakano Sun Mall*

Umemoto Soba (梅もと) – Simple soba and udon joint. *From 290 yen • 6am-10pm*

Kaisen Misakiko (海鮮三崎港) – Super cheap sushi (English menus). *From 90 yen • 11am-11pm*

Furyu (博多風龍) – Tonkotsu (pork) ramen, with free eggs. *From 580 yen • 1am-2am*

Cheap supermarkets (スーパー)

Seiyu has a large supermarket in Nakano Broadway (10am-11pm).

Shopping

100-yen shops

Daiso (ダイソー) – Head out to the back of Nakano Broadway, it's on the left. *10am-10pm*

Pharmacy (ドラッグストア)

Matsumoto, half way up Sun Mall, has tax-free shopping on all the basics (10am-10pm).

How to get there and away

From Shinjuku, take the JR Chuo Line to Nakano (154 yen, 5 mins). It's also just one stop down from Koenji, so you could just walk alongside the track to save some money. Nakano is also on the Metro Tozai Line. *Recommended rail passes: Tokyo Subway Ticket, Tokyo Metro 24-hour Ticket, Tokyo Metropolitan District Pass*

East Tokyo

Akihabara (秋葉原)

Akiba, as they call it here, is a geek's heaven. We are not sure how an area could be more perfect for geeks, from the cosplay girls hanging out on the streets, to the themed restaurants. Anything a geek, or otaku as they say here, needs is available here. For other people, Akihabara is a fascinatingly crazy place with lots of surprises. Shopping and geek experiences are the things to do here. The electronic shops may be cheaper or have slightly later versions of electronic, manga and anime items that you want. Many of the shops have English-speaking staff and goods that can be used abroad. As ever, tax-free options are everywhere.

Walk it and save!
Follow our recommended route on the map, and you will find all the arcades, maid cafes, manga and anime stores, electronic stores and used good stores that you need. Start from either side of the station. Take your time and enjoy the madness!

Things to do

Maids and Maid Cafes (メイドカフェ)
Akihabara is littered with many kinds of maid or cosplay cafes. The best way to see which one is for you, and get any latest deals or discounts, is to walk around the main streets on the map and ask the countless maids what's on offer. They may not speak much English, but will try hard to explain the basics. Ask about the "kabaa chaaji" (cover charge), as this is what often makes the cafes pricey (from around 1000 yen). If they are too pricey for you, you can just walk around and see the cute maids outside. If you take a super cute photo, make sure you post it on Facebook, Instagram or Twitter and mention @SuperCheapJapan!

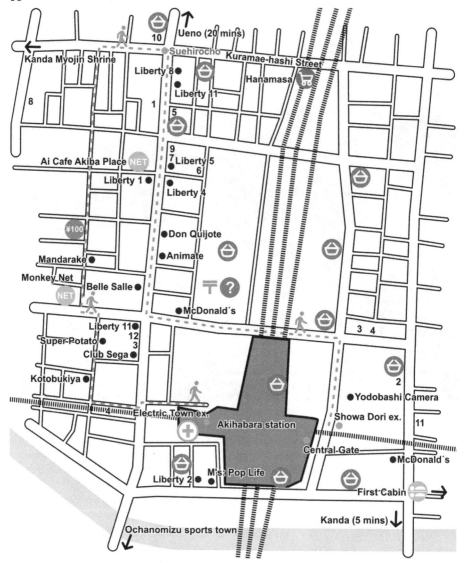

Yodobashi Camera (ヨドバシカメラ)

Possibly the largest electronics shop in Tokyo, a good start to window shopping and people watching in Akihabara. Good choice of products aimed at foreign tourists, but you can often find better prices if you head to the other side of the station, to the electronic shops there. *9:30am-10pm • Outside JR Akihabara station Showa Dori exit*

Chuo Dori

Don Quijote (ドン・キホーテ)

This branch has all the crazy items you would expect to be packed into a Don Quijote, from cheap green tea to cosplay clothes, but also has a large selection of otaku goods. Also has a maid cafe and game arcade. *9am-5pm • Chuo Dori*

Animate (アニメイト)

Another essential for any otaku shopping needs, just be sure to explore all the backstreets and Chuo Dori if you want to get the best price on something expensive. Animate has a large choice of manga, otaku videos and related merchandise. *10am-9pm • Chuo Dori*

Belle Salle Event Space (ベルサール)

Make sure you check out this event space when you are in Akihabara, as there are often free events for the general public. As this is Akiba, they tend to be related to gaming, anime, manga or geek fashion. Ask at the tourist information center for what's on. *Opening times according to event • Up Chuo Dori, just past Club Sega*

Club Sega (クラブ セガ)

One of the many game arcades in Akiba, with a good number of games remaining at 100 yen per play. Also has Purikura, photo booths where guests can have fun customizing and spicing up their pictures. *10am-11:30pm • Large red building on Chuo Dori*

Backstreets

Mandarake Complex (まんだらけ コンプレックス)

Anyone with a nerdy bone in their body will freak out at the awesomeness of this grand complex. Great selection of comics, figures and video games, plus some oddities you would expect from the otaku capital of the world. *12pm-8pm • Head up Chuo Dori, then head left just before Mister Donut and walk two blocks*

Liberty (リバティー)

Second-hand otaku goods. While there is a focus on anime and gaming items, you can find almost anything to satisfy your inner geek. They have various shops across Akihabara, so you can have fun checking them all out as you walk around. *11pm-8pm • Various locations, see map*

Super Potato (スーパーポテト)

A treasure trove of retro gaming and gaming memorabilia. Try out a Virtual Boy, play old school games for a hundred yen in the arcade and check out the retro consoles and games. *11pm-8pm • Behind Club Sega on Chuo Dori*

Kotobukiya (コトブキヤ)

Another great mega store for buying all sorts of Otaku goods, or a perfect bit of window shopping in Akiba. The figurines are of particular interest here. Also has otaku souvenirs, such as character based chocolates and stationery. *10am-8pm • Opposite Super Potato*

M's: Pop Life (大人のデパート エムズ)

Have some fun walking around this high-rise adult store, with items you would never have imagined existed! *10am-11pm • Down street to left of JR Akihabara Electric Town exit*

Kanda Myojin Shrine (神田明神)

A major Shinto shrine near Akihabara and Ueno. More than 1000 years old, the buildings have been stunningly restored and the garden even more so. Japanese visit the shrine to pray, believing that worshipping here will give them luck in family life, business and will even help to find them a partner for marriage. As it's near Akiba, it has also become a kind of guardian for computer data as well, with luck charms on sale for "Protection and Safe keeper of I.T Data". *FREE • 24h • Walk north up Chuo Dori (Akiba's main street) and take the main road left when you get to Suehirocho station. You will see the shrine on the second block after the 7-Eleven convenience store*

100-yen shops

Can Do (キャンドゥ) - Near to Mandarake. *10am-9pm*

Ochanomizu sports town (御茶ノ水スポーツタウン)

The best place in Tokyo to get any kind of sports gear, such as for snowboarding, skiing, hiking or soccer. All tax-free for foreign tourists of course, so seriously consider coming here if you are heading off to the ski resorts or mountains later in your holiday, or even back home. You'll be surprised, and possibly a little overwhelmed, at the number of multi-storey megastores in the area. There are too many to name, so just head along the shopping street and pop into shops that are of interest. Some staff can be a bit pushy, but many can speak a bit of English if needed and will be eager to show you all the discounts on offer. *From Akihabara, you can just walk south of the station, take a right at the crossroad where the main roads meet, then walk down 5 to 10 minutes. The area is also accessible via Ogawamachi station on the Toei Shinjuku Line, Awajicho station on the Marunouchi Line or Shin-Ochanomizu station on the Chiyoda Line. Exit B5 is closest*

Budget food

Budget restaurants on map

1) Mos Burger (モス) - Japanese burgers. *Burgers from 220 yen • 7am-11pm*
2) Matsuya (松屋) - Rice bowls and curry. *Gyudon bowls from 290 yen • 24h*
3) Yoshinoya (吉野家) - Gyudon and curry. *Bowls from 330 yen • 24h*
4) Katsuya (かつや) - Meat cutlet rice bowls. *Bowls from 490 yen • 7am - 11pm*
5) Hidakaya (日高屋) - Ramen and dumplings. *Ramen from 390 yen • 24h*
6) Sukiya (すき家) - Gyudon and curry. *Bowls from 360 yen • 24h*
7) Tempura Tenya (天丼てんや) - Tempura. *Bowls from 500 yen • 11am-11pm*
8) Hotto Motto (ほっともっと) - Bento boxes. *Bentos from 390 yen • 9am-9pm*

Local budget food

9) Mitsuya Soba (小諸そば) - Cheap soba and udon joint, with plastic food outside, so it's easy to choose your bowl. *Soba from 300 yen • Two blocks past Don Quijote on Chou Dori*
10) Taiyaki Kanda Daruma (たいやき神田達磨) - Classic taiyaki (fish-shaped sponge cake with custard or bean filling). *Taiyaki from 250 yen • Just outside Suehirocho station*
11) Coco Ichiban Curry House (カレーハウス CoCo 壱番屋) - The true taste of Japanese curry. *Curry + rice from 500 yen • 24h • Just outside Metro Hibiya exit 1/JR Akihabara Showa Dori exit*
12) Go!Go!CURRY (ゴーゴーカレー) - Darker and richer curry sauce, with some splendidly unhealthy toppings available! *Curry + rice from 530 yen • 10:55am-9:55pm • Next to Club Sega*

Cheap supermarkets (スーパー)

Hanamasa (肉のハナマサ) is a dirt cheap supermarket (24h). To the east of Suehirocho station, along Kuramae-Hashi Dori and under the train tracks.

Pharmacy (ドラッグストア)

Kokumin has a store in Atre Shopping Mall (アトレ), near the Electric Town exit (10am - 9pm).

How to get there and away

From Shinjuku station, take the Sobu Line to Akihabara station (18 mins, 165 yen). From Tokyo station, take the Yamanote line (4 mins, 133 yen). It's also accessible via Akihabara station on the Metro **Hibiya Line**, or via Suehirocho station on the Ginza Line. *Recommended rail passes: Tokyo Subway Ticket, Tokyo Metro 24-hour Ticket, Tokyo Metropolitan District Pass*

Tourist information (観光案内所)

In the UDX building (11am-5:30 pm, closed on Monday).

Ueno (上野)

Ameyoko market, Ueno

Ueno features one of the biggest parks in Tokyo and is one of the main 'cities' within the megalopolis that is Tokyo. There are many museums in the park, and the area is full of brightly lit streets and stores. While it has branches of the main electronic and clothing mega stores, visitors should head to Ameyoko and the park to see what makes Ueno different.

Things to do

Ameyoko (アメ横)

A fascinating collection of streets with many street vendors, Japanese restaurants and game arcades. The atmosphere certainly gets lively here at the weekends, with traders shouting out deals, trying to beat their rivals to get that all important sale. Everything is on sale here of course, such as discount candy, dried fruits, handbags, perfume and watches. Traders will sometimes give you a good bargain, if you are nice! *Take the Shinobazu exit from JR Ueno and follow signs*

Can Do 100-yen store (キャンドゥ)

Walk down Ameyoko and head left at the crossroads with ABC Mart. *10am-9pm*

Ueno park

A huge park, and known as a great place to view the cherry blossoms. Apart from the museums and zoo, free highlights include Bentendo (7am-5pm), an octagonal temple hall, and Toshogu Shrine (9am-4:30pm). Maps are located all over the park, so getting around is easy. *To get there, use the Koen (Park) exit of Ueno station and walk over the road*

Tokyo National Museum (東京国立博物館)

The first stop for anyone with a keen interest in Japanese history, art, design or fashion. It's the oldest national museum in Japan and has by far the richest variety of exhibitions. With more than 110,000 objects and 87 national treasures, you will need at least a few hours to explore the whole complex. *Adults 620 yen, under-18s and over-70s FREE • 9:30am-5pm (closed Mondays and New Year holidays)*

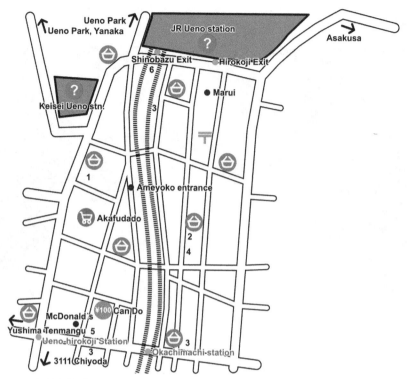

Ueno Zoo (上野動物園)

Tokyo's largest and by far the most popular zoo, especially good for children, but also fun for adults. This is the park containing the famous pandas from China, so be prepared to line up! *Adults 600 yen, children 200 yen, under 12s FREE • 9:30am-5pm (closed Mondays)*

Tokyo Metropolitan Art Museum (東京都美術館)

An awesome museum, largely built underground so as not to stand out too much in the green park. The temporary shows have a vast range of art from across the world, from Van Gogh to Japanese calligraphy. *FREE for main exhibitions • 9:30am-5:30pm (closed every first and third Monday)*

National Museum of Nature and Science (国立科学博物館)

Split into a Japan Gallery and a Global Gallery, this museum thankfully has English explanations for large number of exhibits. As well as having standard exhibitions on dinosaurs and nature, visitors can also learn about the history of humans in Japan and the ecologically diverse islands. Definitely recommended for children, especially as they get in for free. *Adults 620 yen, children FREE • 9am-5pm (closed Mondays and New Year holidays)*

National Museum of Western Art (国立西洋美術館)

Now a World Heritage Site, this museum was designed by Frenchman Le Corbusier in 1959, an influential architect known for heavily influencing 20th century architecture around the world. The museum itself has ever changing exhibitions, so have a peek inside to see if they are of interest to you. *Adults 500 yen, children FREE • 9:30am-5:30pm (closed Mondays and New Year's)*

Yushima Tenmangu Shrine (湯島天満宮)

Devoted to Tenjin, the god of learning, this small Shinto shrine attracts students hoping to boost their chances of exam success. It's a must to come here during the famous plum festival in spring. *FREE • 6am-8pm • 5 mins walk from Ameyoko, see map for directions*

3331 Arts Chiyoda (アーツ千代田 3331)

This complex of mini art galleries is located in an old junior high school. The first floor has a nice café and a play area for the kids, while the second floor has constantly changing displays from a wide variety of Tokyo artists. Occasionally has free workshops on. *FREE • 10am-9pm • Head down Chuo Dori, then take a right at Family Mart and walk down a bit •* http://www.3331.jp/

Travel discounts and packages

The Grutto Pass gives FREE access to the zoo, 100 yen off at the Ueno Royal Museum, 80 yen off the National Museum of Western Art, 100 yen off Tokyo National Museum and 100 yen off special exhibitions at Tokyo Metropolitan Art Museum.

Budget food

Budget restaurants on map

1) Matsuya (松屋) - Rice bowls and curry. *Gyudon bowls from 290 yen • 24h*
2) Ringer Hut (リンガーハット) - Fish ramen. *Ramen from 630 yen • 10am-2am*
3) Oedo Sushi (大江戸寿司) - Conveyor belt sushi. *Sushi from 140 yen • 11:30am-11:20pm*
4) Hidakaya (日高屋) - Ramen and gyoza dumplings. *Ramen from 390 yen • 10am-3am*
5) Yoshinoya (吉野家) - Gyudon and curry. *Bowls from 330 yen • 24h*
6) Tsuruya (つるや) - Cheap soba and udon. *Soba from 290 yen • 4:30am-1am*

Ameyoko

There are lots of small stalls and shops selling fruits, ice creams and deep fried snacks for 100-300 yen each. Larger takeout meals (such as Japanese pancakes, kebabs and noodles) are around 400-500 yen, so this is a great spot for budget travelers. Be sure to explore the interconnecting streets for a few gems and special offers as well.

Cheap supermarkets (スーパー)

Akafudado (赤札堂) has a branch in the AbAb (アブアブ) shopping mall (10am-9pm). Note that Ameyoko also has plenty of stalls selling items like fruits, vegetables and cheap takeouts.

Water bottle refill spots

The park has some water fountains, or go to the chain restaurants.

Pharmacy (ドラッグストア)

Plenty of drug stores are open late on Ameyoko.

How to get there and away

From Shinjuku station, take the JR Yamanote Line to Ueno station (25 mins, 194 yen). From Tokyo station, take the JR Yamanote Line to Ueno station (6 mins, 154 yen). Ueno is also on the Tokyo Metro Hibiya and Ginza lines. *Recommended rail passes: Tokyo Subway Ticket, Tokyo Metro 24-hour Ticket, Tokyo Metropolitan District Pass*

Walk it and save!

Asakusa is a nice city walk from Ueno, via Kappabashi. We recommend starting with Ueno in the morning, then strolling over to Asakusa in the early evening/late afternoon. Check the map for the road to go down. After about 30 minutes you will get to Asakusa.

Tourist information (観光案内所)

Located at both the JR Ueno (9:15am-5:15pm) and Keisei Ueno (9:30am-6:30pm) stations.

Yanaka (谷中)

Small, adorable shops lining the streets of Yanaka

One of the few areas in Tokyo to be spared by bombing in WW2, Yanaka is a nostalgic neighborhood near Ueno. Full of lots of narrow, winding lanes and mom-and-pop shops, it's a welcome break from the modernity of most of Tokyo and a good spot for a free stroll. The area is well known for wood carvings, textiles and the like, so it a nice spot for unique gifts.

Things to do

Yanaka Ginza

Head down the main street to see what old Tokyo was really like. The area doesn't have modern buildings like all the areas around it, and has more than 50 tiny, community run shops.

Snack stalls and shops

These local establishments sell old-school finger food and other snacks, with prices from around just 50 yen, to a staggering 180 yen for a pink rice candy! There are also shops selling super cheap Manju buns. These rice buns come in a variety of flavors, such as green tea or peach. You'll get some great pictures, so be sure to post them on Twitter, Instagram or Facebook and mention @SuperCheapJapan to share them with the world!

Shinimonogurui (しにものぐるい)

Get your own personal stamp, called a Hanko, at this unique store. While traditional stamps are used for business and such, this store creates customized stamps with cute characters and your name in Japanese. Get one for yourself or bring back a very unique souvenir! *From 2600 yen • 10:30-6pm (closed Tuesdays) • 5 minutes from Nippori station on Yanaka Ginza*

Can Do

Local branch of the famous 100-yen store chain, with some extras for the tourists in town.

Free sample food and drink

Keep an eye out on the food stalls, as a few sometimes hand out free samples of traditional Japanese confectionery. Some of the tea shops, such as Kinyoshien (金吉園), opposite the 100-yen shop, offers complimentary green tea to shoppers (10am-7pm).

Yanaka Cemetery (谷中霊園)

With the Skytree looming in the distance, the cemetery is quite a spot. While visiting a cemetery may not seem so exciting, there are some spectacular tombstone and pillars, as well as a five-storey pagoda. Also a great spot for cherry blossoms. *FREE • 24h • South of Nippori*

Space Oguraya (すぺーす小倉屋)

Another spot that shows off Yanaka's community spirit is this cool little arts and crafts gallery. Now registered as an official cultural property, it houses a selection of Japanese pottery, ink prints and wood carving. *FREE • 10:30am-4:30pm • Heading south into the cemetery, take a right at the crossroad on the main road (look out for the police box). Take the first left after exiting, and the gallery is just on the left side*

Nezu Shrine (根津神社)

Small shrine complex and garden, famous for its yearly Azalea Festival and lane of small red 'tori' gates. In early April to early May it has around 3000 azaleas and is well worth the visit. *FREE • 9am-5pm • 5 mins south from Sendagi station, use station maps to get your bearings*

Budget food

Matsuya (松屋) - rice bowls and curry. *Gyudon bowls from 290 yen • 24h • Outside Sendagi station*
Mister Donut (ミスタードーナツ) - Donuts and cheap light meals. *Donuts from 100 yen • 8am-11pm • Outside Sendagi station*
Tempura Tenya (天丼てんや) - Deep-fried fish and vegetables. *Bowls from 500 yen • 11am-11pm • To the right of Nippori station east exit*
Hidakaya (日高屋) - Ramen and dumplings. *Ramen from 390 yen • 24h • Down the road from Tenya*
Toohoo (トーホー) - Cheap bentos and snacks, with friendly service. *Bentos from 380 yen, snacks from 120 yen • 10am-6pm • On the corner of Yanaka Ginza shopping street, near the information center*

Cheap supermarkets (スーパー)

There is a MyBasket (まいばすけっと) minimart on the main shopping street (7am-12pm).

How to get there and away

Head to Sendagi on the Chiyoda line to start at the south end, or Nippori station on the JR Yamanote Line for the north end. Large information maps outside the stations make it easy to walk to Yanaka in a few minutes. Ueno Park is a five-minute walk south of Yanaka Cemetery. *Recommended rail passes: Tokyo Subway Ticket, Tokyo Metro 24-hour Ticket*

Tourist information (観光案内所)

The Yanesen Tourist Info & Culture Centre (9:30am-5pm, http://www.ti-yanesen.jp/) is an excellent place to get more info on the area. They also offer cultural experiences, such as enjoying a cooking class with a local, calligraphy classes and Japanese lessons for tourists.

Imperial Palace area (皇居東御苑と東京駅)

While the area around Tokyo station is expensive real estate, with shop and restaurant prices to reflect that, there are some essential stops for budget travelers. The Imperial Palace East Garden is a highlight for many in Tokyo, and there are a few other free spots to check out in the area. Just forget that the land value of the area used to be more valuable than the whole of California's, take in the modern city sights and take plenty of photos.

Hama Rikyu Garden, near the Imperial Palace

Travel discounts and packages

Tokyo Station Area Art Gallery Map (東京駅周辺美術館共通券)

Get 100 yen off at five galleries around Tokyo station. Just pick up the map from one of the galleries or the information center and bring it with you to each one. The discounts work at Tokyo Station Gallery, Bridgestone Museum of Art, Idemitsu Museum of Arts, Mitsui Memorial Museum and Mitsubishi Ichigokan Museum. Also consider the Grutto Pass, though, if you want to see even more than these ones.

Things to do

Tokyo station

Imperial Palace East Garden (皇居東御苑)

The East Garden, right in the center of Tokyo, is a free park within the Imperial Palace complex. First opened to the public in 1968, the 210,000 square meters garden has a variety of interesting spots. Highlights include the Honmaru castle compound, one of the last remaining Edo period gardens in Ninomaru, and the remains of the former castle tower. The free Museum of the Imperial Collections (Sannomaru-Shōzōkan) contains 9,500 items of Imperial art, such as paintings and calligraphy artifacts. *FREE • 9am-4:30pm (closed Monday and Friday) • Near Otemachi station exit C10, which is connected to Tokyo station by underground passage*

Tokyo Character Street (東京キャラクターストリート)

Plenty of free samples to be had here. This underground shopping mall has more than 20 stores, all themed after well-known characters in Japanese comics, manga, games, music and on TV. They have everyone covered, from Hello Kitty to Rilakkuma to Doraemon. There is also a pop-up shop area called 'Ichiban Plaza', which has various themed stalls open. *FREE • 10am-10:30pm • Near JR Tokyo station Yaesu Underground central exit and Daimaru Dept. Store*

Walk it and save!

The most famous walking or jogging route for any Tokyoite is to go around the whole grounds of the Imperial Palace. It's a pretty simple, flat route and the scenery along the way is a perfect mix of tall skyscrapers, greenery and downtown city life. Start by walking from the west side of Tokyo station, and once you get to the moat just head around in either direction. *Time required: 2-3 hours • Difficulty: Easy*

Shimbashi

Hama Rikyu Garden (浜離宮)

Japan's premier garden, you may not need to visit another after this one. The garden has two parts, the southern part which was a villa for feudal lords in the 17th to 19th centuries and the more modern northern garden. On the south end, an area originally used as hunting grounds for the shogun ruler of Japan has been reborn. Now Shio-iri-no Niwa, it's a splendid Japanese garden on the sea, and also has a waterbus to Asakusa and Odaiba. *300 yen • 9am-5pm • From Shimbashi, follow signs to Shiodome, then to the garden (behind Conrad Tokyo hotel / コンラッド東京)*

Advertising Museum Tokyo (アド・ミュージアム)

A surprisingly interesting (and free!) museum, showcasing Japanese advertising over the centuries. From Kimono ladies selling beer to retro packaging, the museum is a fascinating change from the usual museums in Tokyo. *FREE • 11am-6pm (Closed Sundays, Mondays and holidays) • Take the subway to Shiodome station (Oedo Line or Yurikamome Line) or Shimbashi (JR Yamanote, Ginza and Asakusa lines). Follow the signs underground to Caretta Shiodome*

Kyu Shiba Rikyu Garden (旧芝離宮恩賜庭園)

More compact and a bit cheaper than Hama Rikyu, this is an old feudal lord's garden. A very Japanese traditional garden, set around a pond with carefully placed rocks and trees. *Adults 150 yen, children FREE • 9am-5pm • Take the subway to Hamamatsucho station on the Monorail or JR Yamanote Line, or Daimon station on the Oedo and Asakusa lines. Also a short walk south of Hama Rikyu*

Budget food

Tokyo station itself, plus the area around is mainly filled up with overpriced restaurants and bakeries. It's therefore highly recommended to eat elsewhere or bring food with you. Shimbashi is a similar case, but there are a few chain restaurants outside the station if you are desperate to sit down and eat. Otherwise head straight to the convenience stores for a cheap bento or cup noodle.

Water bottle refill spots

There are occasional water fountains in the parks and gardens.

Pharmacy (ドラッグストア)

Matsumoto-Kiyoshi (マツモトキヨシ) is in the Yaesu underground mall (8am-9pm).

How to get there and away

There are more than a dozen JR and Metro lines to Tokyo station, so check at your nearest station for the quickest route. For Shimbashi, take the JR **Yamanote Line** (133 yen, 4 mins) from Tokyo station, or the Asakusa or Ginza subway lines. *Recommended rail passes: Tokyo Subway Ticket, Tokyo Metro 24-hour Ticket, Tokyo Metropolitan District Pass*

Tourist information (観光案内所)

In the Marunouchi Trust Tower, just to the right after using the Nihonbashi exit (10am-7pm).

Asakusa (浅草)

Asakusa, with the Skytree in the distance

Asakusa is the main tourist zone in Tokyo, a bustling area full of tourists from across the world. While this may put some travelers off, it is still a must see for any first-time visitor to Japan. Asakusa features Tokyo's most famous temple, atmospheric old-fashioned streets and plenty of free things to do for budget travelers.

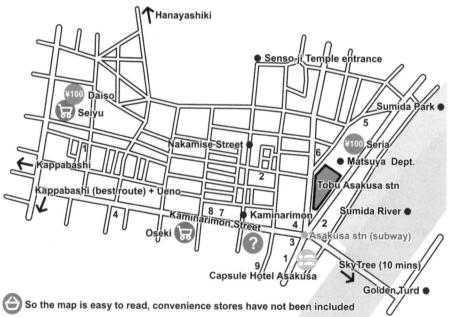

There is both a Tobu Asakusa station, as well as the combined Tokyo Metro and Toei Subway underground section. To get your bearings from the underground, head for exit 1,2 or 3, which all bring you out on Kaminarimon Dori (street), the main street on the map.

Things to do

Asakusa

Senso-ji Temple (浅草寺)
Tokyo's most famous and popular temple. One of the oldest in Tokyo, founded in 628. The Asakusa Kannon deity (goddess of mercy) was enshrined here, so many believe visiting the temple will bring good fortune to all. Be sure to walk around the whole complex, including the five-storey pagoda, as there is lots to see apart from the main buildings. Walking around the temple complex in the evening is also rather impressive. *FREE • Grounds 24h, main hall 6am-5pm (until 6:30pm Oct - Mar) • Through Kaminarimon and down five mins*

Kaminarimon (雷門)
Get your selfie stick out for Tokyo's premier selfie spot. The 'Thunder Gate' features statues of Raijin, god of thunder, and Fujin, god of wind. The giant lantern hanging below is probably the most photographed in Japan. *FREE • Down Kaminarimon Dori from Asakusa (Tokyo Metro) station exits 1,2,3*

Nakamise Street (仲見世通り)
Asakusa is full of interesting shops for a bit of window shopping and the occasional purchase! Many of the streets look like Tokyo of the past. Take your time here, as you may be able to watch stall owners make traditional Japanese sweets, such as Ningyoyaki (Japanese snack cakes), which you can buy for 100 yen or so after. As this is the main tourist destination in Tokyo, prices can be high around the main temple and nearby streets. There are plenty of cheaper spots outside this main tourist zone. *Between Kaminarimon and Senso-ji Temple*

Sumida Park and River (墨田公園・墨田川)
A quiet park along the river, and a good place to chill out for a bit or enjoy a bento. A must see during the cherry blossom season. *East of Asakusa station*

The Golden Turd (金のうんこ)
OK, so this is not the official name, but the Asahi Beer HQ and hall does look like it has a golden poo on top. This odd resemblance was apparently due to the architects drinking a few too many beers in a meeting, and it's one of those must take photos of Tokyo. *Sumida River*

Hanayashiki Amusement Park (浅草花やしき)
The oldest amusement park in Japan, this nostalgic experience is fun for all the family. *Admission 1000 yen, ride tickets 100 yen each • 10am-6pm • Short walk west of Senso-ji Temple*

Free sample food

Matsuya (松屋浅草)
One of the poshest department stores in Tokyo has a large food court offering a good variety of free snacks, drinks and more to try out. Particularly well known for old-school Japanese confectionery. *10am-8pm • Connected to Tobu Asakusa station*

Kappabashi (合羽橋)
True oddball tourism here. Fascinating street for restaurant and cafe owners to buy specialist goods, almost anything you could want for your kitchen can be found here. Merchants first started selling goods here as far back as 1912, and the area now has more than 170 specialist shops. From plastic food to furniture to ovens to cutlery, Kappabashi is worth checking out for

an hour or two. Plus, as this is an area for restaurant owners, the prices for items such as cutlery can be very cheap. The plastic food models can often be cheaper in shops like Tokyu Hands in Shibuya or Shinjuku though. *Tawaramachi station on Ginza Line*

Walk it and save: Asakusa to Kappabashi

From Asakusa station (Tokyo Metro) exits 1,2,3 or Asakusa Culture and Tourism Center, head down Kaminarimon Street in the opposite direction of Sumida river. Take a left turn at the end of the road and walk down to Tawaramachi station. Take a right turn, then Kappabashi is four blocks down on the right.

Budget food

Budget restaurants on map

1) **Matsuya (松屋) -** Rice bowls and curry. *Gyudon bowls from 290 yen • 24h*
2) **Ganzo Sushi (元祖寿司) -** Conveyor belt sushi. *Sushi from 125 yen • 11am-9:30pm*
3) **Fuji Soba (富士そば) -** Soba, udon and curry. *Soba from 300 yen • 24h*
4) **Hidakaya (日高屋) -** Ramen and dumplings. *Ramen from 390 yen • 24h*
5) **Mos Burger (モス) -** Japanese burgers. *Burgers from 220 yen • 7am-10pm*
6) **Yoshinoya (吉野家) -** Gyudon and curry. *Bowls from 330 yen • 24h*

Local budget food

There are some basic soba, udon and set meal restaurants on Kaminarimon Street, as well as these highlights:

7) **Arashi Ramen (らあめん花月嵐) -** Inventive seasonal soups and toppings. *Ramen from 780 yen • 11am-2am • Kaminarimon Street*
8) **Sushizanmai (すしざんまい) -** Conveyor belt sushi, good for a cheap light meal. *Sushi plates from 108 yen • 24h • Kaminarimon Street*
9) **Origin Dining (オリジンダイニング) –** Japanese set meals. *Sets from 580 yen • 11am-11:30pm • Down narrow street on left at exit 2 on Kaminarimon Street*

Cheap supermarkets (スーパー)

Best option is the Seiyu supermarket in ROX shopping mall (24h). Ozeki supermarket is closer to the station on Kaminarimon Street (9:30am-9pm).

Shopping

100-yen shops

Seria (セリア) - Inside the Tobu Asakusa station complex. *10am-8pm*
Daiso (ダイソー) - Inside the ROX shopping mall. *10am-8pm*

Pharmacy (ドラッグストア)

Matsukiyo Papasu (どらっぐぱぱす) has a shop on Kaminarimon street (10am-10pm).

How to get there and away

Asakusa is on the Tokyo Metro Ginza Line, Toei Asakusa Line and the starting point for Tobu trains to Nikko. From Shinjuku station, take the Marunouchi Line to Akasaka-mitsuke, then the Ginza Line to Asakusa station (30 mins, 237 yen). From Tokyo station, take the Marunouchi Line to Ginza, then take the Ginza Line to Asakusa station (25 mins, 200 yen). *Recommended rail passes: Tokyo Subway Ticket, Tokyo Metro 24-hour Ticket*

Tourist information (観光案内所)

One of the best equipped and staffed in Tokyo, the Asakusa Culture and Tourism Center is just outside Asakusa (Tokyo Metro) station exit 2 (9am-8pm).

Skytree (東京スカイツリー)

The Tokyo Skytree is the tallest tower in the world, at 634 meters in height. With all the new skyscrapers popping up over the last few decades Tokyo Tower was just not tall enough anymore, and a new broadcast tower was needed. The neofuturistic design and computer animated illuminations at night make this tower stand out from all the rest.

At the base of the tower is Tokyo Solamachi, a huge shopping mall. The number of shops is just astonishing, and there are all sorts of fun themed areas. The Japanese Souvenirs area (4F) has loads of unique gifts on sale, the Japan Experience Zone (5F) has some fun, very Japanese interactive games and experiences, while Fashion Zone (2F) has plenty of tax-free clothing shops and more. There are also some 'character shops', offering toys and souvenirs based around your favorite TV, anime and manga characters.

Things to do

Head up the tower

Already been up the free Metropolitan building in Shinjuku and want to go a little higher, up the tallest building in Japan? The first observation deck is 350-m high, while the upper observation deck is all the way up at 450-m. It's a superb view, and even more fun walking over the glass floors, if you have the guts! A great option for international visitors is the Fast Skytree Ticket, which allows you to skip the first line. Buy these at the dedicated counter on the fourth floor, near the west entrance. *Adults from 2060 yen (plus 1030 yen for upper deck), children from 620 yen • 8am-10pm (last admission at 9pm) •* http://www.tokyo-skytree.jp/en/

Free sample food

Head to Tokyo Solamachi to try your luck at some free food samples. The best spot is Food Marche (2F), which has various counters offering different tastes from across the world. Also worth trying is Solamachi Shotengai (1F), which has some amazing cheesecake and biscuit shops giving out free samples to potential customers.

Budget food

The restaurants in Solamachi and up in the tower aren't generally aimed at budget travelers, but as mentioned there are lots of places to get some free grub, plus the odd chain restaurant. Life Supermarket is just across the road from the east side of the complex (9am-12am).

Water bottle refill spots

Head up to the food court in Tokyo Solamachi to fill up your water bottle.

How to get there and away

From Asakusa, take the **Oedo Line** to Oshiage station (4 mins, 174 yen). You can also use the Tobu **Skytree Line** or the Metro **Hanzomon Line**. Note that you can save a bit of money by walking to the Skytree from Asakusa. It's just a short 10-minute walk to the tower.
Recommended rail passes: Tokyo Subway Ticket, Tokyo Metro 24-hour Ticket

Kiyosumi Garden area (清澄庭園エリア)

Not often visited by foreign tourists, it's worth mentioning this area for those wanting to get away from the more crowded gardens and museums of central Tokyo.

Kiyosumi Garden (清澄庭園)

The former residence of an Edo period business magnate, Kiyosumi Garden is a compact but beautifully traditional Japanese garden. Featuring rocks and structures brought in from across Japan, it's a quick visit and is also cheaper than most gardens, such as Hama Rikyu Garden. *Adults 150 yen, children FREE • 9am-5pm • Kiyosumi-shirakawa Station on the Metro Hanzomon and Toei Oedo lines • Recommended rail passes: Tokyo Subway Ticket, Tokyo Metro 24-hour Ticket*

Fukagawa Edo museum (深川江戸資料館)

It's also worth checking out this small museum, which has recreated what Tokyo would have looked like in the Edo period. The buildings inside were built using old traditional techniques by some very dedicated volunteers. English info is sometimes lacking, so the Edo-Tokyo Museum in Ryogoku may be better for some. *Adults 400 yen, children 40 yen • 9am-5pm • Follow maps from station exit A3 (5 minutes on foot)*

Ryogoku (両国)

Ryogoku is a great choice for budget travelers, with a few free tourist sites that could easily take up a day. Home to the sumo tournaments in Tokyo, the area has the traditional atmosphere of old Tokyo.

Things to do

Edo-Tokyo Museum

A massive museum about the history of Tokyo, and its predecessor Edo. Features replicas and originals from as far back as the Edo era (between 1603 and 1868), a detailed timeline of the city and art from different periods. It will definitely take up at least half a day to see it all, so it's great value for money. Excellent English descriptions available. *Adults 600 yen, children and seniors 300 yen (FREE with Grutto Pass) • 9:30am-5:30pm (Saturday until 7:30pm). Closed Mondays • Just outside Ryogoku station •* http://www.edo-tokyo-museum.or.jp/en/

Sumo Museum (相撲博物館)

Created to show off the rich heritage of sumo in Ryogoku, and in Japan, and to preserve this for future fans of Japan's national sport. The museum has a host of displays showing the history of sumo, such as ceremonial aprons worn by various fighters and official rankings over the years. *FREE • 10am-4:30pm (closed weekends, national holidays) • Just outside Ryogoku station*

Watch the Sumo tournaments at Kokugikan (両国国技館)

A truly awesome experience, watching sumo really blew our socks off! Even if you don't speak Japanese, watching the fights and the ceremony around them in this all-day show will be one of your most culturally rewarding experiences in Japan. The grand, purpose-built stadium has enough traditional elements to keep the experience authentic, but all the modern facilities and takeaway joints a budget traveler needs. Just book as early as possible, otherwise prices can go sky high! *Tickets from 3800 yen (book and check schedule at* http://www.sumo.or.jp/EnTicket*) • January, May, September (two dates in each month)*

Watch Sumo wrestlers train for free at Arashio Stable (荒汐部屋)

Is around 4000 yen too much to pay for a bit of Sumo? One option is to see the sumo wrestlers train in the morning for their big tournaments. This shows another side of the Sumo wrestlers' lives and provides a fascinating insight into Japan's national sport. Note that viewers do not actually go inside the training area, but watch via a window outside. *FREE • 7:30am-10:00am most days (except March, July and November) • Check the day before at* http://www.arashio.net/

Former Yasuda Garden (旧安田庭園)

A medium sized traditional Japanese garden with great views of the SkyTree, and one of the prettiest free ones around. Built during the Genroku period (1688 - 1703), it feels like a miniature version of more famous Japanese gardens. The garden is also a nice place to check out for the cherry blossoms or autumn colors. *FREE • 9am-4:30pm • Just behind the Sumo Museum, towards Sumida river*

Yokoamicho Park (横網町公園)

We were a little bit surprised to come across this peaceful park nearby, with its huge greenish pagoda-like temple. Also features memorials and gardens dedicated to those lost in earthquakes, Japan's constant menace. *FREE • 24h • Opposite back entrance/exit of Yasuda Garden*

Volunteer guides and tours

Edo-Tokyo Museum Volunteer Guides

Free tours of the permanent exhibition, which take about two hours. Head to the 6th floor Voluntary Guide Desk or a ticket counter to see if you can join a group. Two weeks' notice is advised, but if you can't do this, there is no harm in asking!

Travel discounts and packages

The Grutto Pass can be used to get free access to the Edo-Tokyo Museum, as well as to receive 20% off special exhibits.

Budget food

The best street to head for cheap food is the one on the south side of Ryogoku station. Here are some highlights, from west to east:

Saint Marc (サンマルクカフェ) - Not super cheap, but sells reasonably priced croissants and coffee. Also has a free water fountain. *Croissants from 120 yen • 7am-11pm*

Saizeriya (サイゼリヤ) - Light Italian dishes, such as a small pizza or pasta dish, this is a good spot. *Pizzas from 390 yen, pasta from 399 yen • 10am-12am*

Matsuya (松屋) - Gyudon and burgers. *Meals from 290 yen • 24h*

Hidakaya (日高屋) - Cheap ramen chain. *Ramen from 390 yen • 24h*

Kojiro Ramen (ラーメン餃子館 小次郎) - A more down to earth, old school gyoza dumplings and ramen joint. *Ramen from 580 yen • 11am-4am*

Hinoya Curry (日乃屋カレー) - Old school Japanese curry restaurant, with decently sized portions. *Curry rice from 730 yen • 11am-10pm*

Cheap supermarkets (スーパー)

There is a reasonably priced Maruetsu Petit (マルエツ プチ) supermarket (24h). Go to the Oedo Line station, and head out exit A5, then walk down in the opposite direction of the overhead tracks and to the left at the main road. It's across the road two blocks down.

How to get there and away

From Shinjuku station, take the Sobu Line to Ryogoku station (16 mins, 216 yen). From Tokyo station, take the Yamanote Line to Akihabara station, then the Sobu Line to Ryogoku station (9 mins, 154 yen). *Recommended rail passes: Tokyo Metropolitan District Pass, Tokyo Subway Ticket*

Tourist information (観光案内所)

Inside Ryogoku station (west side), open 10am-6pm.

Ginza (銀座)

You may have not been expecting to see Ginza in a budget travel guide, but times are changing. While Ginza has a reputation as the place only the rich can enjoy, the rise of budget-conscious customers in Japan has changed Ginza a lot in the last few years. There are some bargains to be had! It's worth visiting this shopping street for an hour or two.

Things to do

Watch Kabuki at Kabukiza (歌舞伎座)

Kabuki is the most famous form of Japanese theater. Featuring beautiful costumes and some very Japanese sets, the male-only performers make a strong use of body language and color to express themselves in the story. Normal tickets for a whole performance are very pricey, so if you want to save money go for the single act tickets, called Makumi. They are more than enough for tourists who want to experience Kabuki in the flesh. Note these can only be bought on the day of performance at the theater, so check the schedule on their website. *Usually 800-2000 yen (Makumi) • Various times, check website • Higashi-Ginza station exit 3, walkable via underground passage from Ginza station •* https://www.kabukiweb.net/

Ginza Dori

The following shops and galleries are listed in order, as you approach from Ginza station exits A2 or A4, heading south (look out for Uniqlo and Ginza Six shopping mall):

Maison Hermes gallery
Head straight past the crazily expensive items in this shop and head up to the top floor to see some fancy art. It has new artists on display every month or so, showing off their latest pieces. Often has art that will be of interest to kids too. Shiseido, down the road, also has its own free gallery. *FREE • 11am-8pm • Outside Ginza station, exit B7 •* http://www.maisonhermes.jp/en/ginza/

Uniqlo
This branch of the budget clothing retailer made quite a splash when it opened in Ginza. Featuring 12 floors of cheap clothes, shoes and more, it also boasts multilingual staff and the latest fashions for this fancy area. Nearby GU is similar, but even cheaper. *11am-9pm*

LOAX Tax-free
Specializing in tax-free items for tourists, you can get a good bargain on bags, watches and electronics that can be used abroad. *11am-8pm • 5F and 6F of ExitMelsa, after GU*

Ginza Six
It's another expensive shopping mall, but this new complex has multiple art installations from renowned modern artist Yayoi Kusama, which you can have a look at for free. Her colorful and imaginative art is worth a peek inside the mega-mall. *10:30am-8:30pm*

Hakuhinkan Toy Park (博品館トイパーク)
One of Tokyo's best novelty and toy stores, a great choice for kids and big kids alike. A huge selection of both modern and nostalgic toys are on offer at this multi-storey complex. Also has tax-free shopping. *11am-8pm • On the right, just before you get to the express way*

Budget food

There is not much here for a cheap meal, so best to eat somewhere else, unless you see a good deal. On the other hand, Hanamasa (肉のハナマサ) is a dirt-cheap supermarket if you want to make your own food (24h). Head south down Ginza Dori, the main road, for about 10 minutes past Uniqlo to the expressway. Hanamasa is on the left, under the expressway.

How to get there and away

Ginza station is on the Ginza, Hibiya and Marunouchi Metro lines. It can also be accessed via the underground passageway from Yurakucho station on the JR Yamanote Line or Metro Yurakucho line. You can also save on the ticket by walking south from Tokyo station (10 mins). *Recommended rail passes: Tokyo Subway Ticket, Tokyo Metro 24-hour Ticket*

South Tokyo

Odaiba (お台場)

Rainbow Bridge and Tokyo as seen from Odaiba at night

Set to be the main site of the 2020 Olympic Village, Odaiba is heading for some big changes. This man-made island was built during the boom economy in the 1980s, but when the bubble burst it was left to become a bit of a ghost town. The city has since opened up Odaiba to entertainment and shopping complexes, and the main area has been reborn as Tokyo's favorite date spot. Companies such as Fuji TV, with its futuristic HQ, and others have slowly moved into the area, creating an often vibrant waterfront. In the summer, come on the weekends as there are often free events or festivals on. Ask at a tourist information center for what's on.

Things to do

Odaiba Seaside Park (お台場海浜公園)

A nice place to take a stroll, with views of Tokyo city to the north. Come at night to take photos of the small Statue of Liberty (展望広場) replica, or chill out on the artificial beach in the daytime. *FREE • 24h • North of Odaiba-kaihinkoen and Tokyo Teleport stations*

Gundam Statue (ガンダム)

Mega statue of a Gundam robot, similar to Transformers in the west. Steam rushes out of the beast's vents in the evening. Immensely awesome! *FREE • 24h • Outside Diver City Tokyo Plaza*

Oedo-Onsen Monogatari Hot Spring (大江戸温泉物語)

Oedo Onsen Monogatari is an amazing hot spring, with various types of baths (including some lukewarm ones for beginners), Japanese restaurants and other lighthearted attractions. It's almost like a hot spring theme park. Included in the price is the rental of Yukatas (traditional Japanese robes), so visitors can walk around an Edo (old Tokyo) themed town! The Japanese section of its website often has discount coupons, so ask someone who can read Japanese to check before if you can't. *Adults 2720 yen (Sat & Sun 2936 yen) (500 yen discount after 6pm), children 1058 yen • 11am-9am • On south side, next to Telecom Center station*

Panasonic Center / Risupia (パナソニックセンター)

This free exhibition shows off Panasonic's latest technology and prototypes for the future, including a 'home of the future'. Not essential, but worth a visit if you have time, especially if you have kids whose time you need to occupy. *FREE • 10am-5pm • Near Kokusai-Tenjijo station. Walk over Yumenoo Bridge (夢の大橋) and straight down 10 minutes*

Tokyo Rinkai Disaster Prevention Park (東京臨海広域防災公園)

Fascinating for adults as well as older kids, the purpose of this museum is to prepare people for an earthquake. Beginning with a simulation of an earthquake, guests then navigate a realistic simulated disaster zone. *FREE • 9:30am-5pm • A few minutes past Panasonic Center*

Miraikan Museum of Emerging Science and Innovation (日本科学未来館)

A more in-depth technology showcase, this is the place to interact with the latest robots from companies such as Honda or Sony, with creations such as Asimo making appearances in the past. The museum has all the latest emerging technology from this tech-crazy country, with excellent English explanations provided in the vast exhibitions. *Adults 620 yen, children 210 yen • 10am-5pm (closed on Tuesday and New Year holidays) • Just north of Telecom Center station*

Toyota City Showcase (トヨタ シティ ショウケース)

Test drive the latest Toyota models and learn about the latest in automotive technology. The History Garage has more than 60 cars from across the generations, plus children can learn traffic rules while having a drive of their own 'petit cars'. *FREE • 11am-9pm • Inside Palette Town*

Shopping malls

Tokyo Teleport station in Odaiba is surrounded by several large shopping malls, all of which are great for window shopping or photo taking, but don't generally have any great deals or discounts compared to places such as Harajuku or Shinjuku. These are the best for budget travelers:

Palette Town (パレットタウン)

Huge complex, with a variety of themed zones and a Ferris wheel as well. Definitely check out Venus Port, which is a rather strange shopping center, supposed to look like some kind of grand Italian city, but all inside for convenience of course. *11am-9pm • Outside Aomi station*

Decks Tokyo Beach (デックス東京ビーチ)

Street performers show off their skills for free at the decking area outside this shopping mall. Inside is the rather expensive Sega Joypolis indoor theme park, but Daiba 1-chome Shoutengai on the second floor is full of fascinating knickknacks, retro souvenirs and cheap retro games to play. Top spot for odd souvenirs to take home. *11am-9pm • Between Tokyo Teleport station and Odaiba Seaside Park*

Diver City Tokyo Plaza (ダイバーシティ東京 プラザ)

Another large complex, the highlight being the above-mentioned Gundam statue outside. Apart from that, there are a host of chain stores including a branch of budget clothes manufacturer Uniqlo. *10am-9pm • Few mins west of Tokyo Teleport station*

100-yen shops

Seria (セリア) - Inside Venus Port in Palette Town. *11am-9pm*
Daiso (ダイソー) - Inside Diver City. *10am-9pm*

Pharmacy (ドラッグストア)

Decks Tokyo Beach has a Matsumotokiyoshi pharmacy (マツモトキヨシ) (10am - 9pm).

Budget food

It's generally a very touristy area, so prices tend to be high. There are some fun themed areas to enjoy, though.

Tokyo Ramen Stadium (東京ラーメン国技館)

Stuff yourself with all kinds of ramen, from soy sauce to pork to full-on chili red ramen. Six of the best ramen chefs in the country have come together to create this very tasty experience. *Ramen from 980 yen • 11am-11pm • Aquacity (next to Decks Tokyo Beach) 5F*

Takoyaki Museum

If you are a fan of takoyaki (octopus balls), then this is the place for you. Features some much loved stalls from Osaka selling their local variants, plus shops to buy kits to make them yourselves. *Takoyaki from around 600 yen • 10am-9pm • Diver City Tokyo Plaza*

Cheap supermarkets (スーパー)

Although there are numerous convenience stores around, Maruetsu (マルエツ) has a larger range at its supermarket outside Odaiba-kaihinkoen station (9am - 10pm).

Water bottle refill spots

There is free Japanese tea and water in Oedo-Onsen Monogatari, but not many water fountains around.

How to get there and away

By free shuttle bus (大江戸温泉物語へのシャトルバス)

If you are going to or coming back from Oedo-Onsen Monogatari Hot Spring, there are free shuttle buses from/to many locations across Tokyo. These include Shinjuku, Shinagawa station, Tokyo station, Tokyo Teleport station and Sumiyoshi. Timetables and pickup points change frequently, so check at http://daiba.ooedoonsen.jp/en/ the day before you go or ask at your accommodation or a tourist information center. Shinagawa station has the most frequent service, but there are plenty of options.

By rail

From Shinjuku station, take the **Saikyo Line** to Osaki station, then the **Rinkai Line** to Tokyo Teleport (24 mins, 494 yen). Some **Saikyo Line** trains continue from Osaki on the **Rinkai Line**, so there is no need to change. From Tokyo station, take the Keiyo Line to Shin-Kiba station, then the **Rinkai Line** to Tokyo Teleport (22 mins, 432 yen). You can also take the **Yurikamome Line** from Shimbashi to Daiba station (14 mins, 319 yen).

Tourist information (観光案内所)

Just outside the Tokyo Teleport station gates is 'Odaiba Sky Tourist Information' (10am - 6pm). Free wifi and charging points are available to use.

Fish markets

The outer market at Tsukiji Market

For many generations, tourists flocked to Tsukiji Market to see the entertaining theater of the fish wholesale market. But times are changing, and it was finally decided several years ago to build a new market in nearby Toyosu. Sushi and sashimi lovers may want to go to both, to experience both the charm of the old one and the variety of the new one, but most tourists should be content with the huge new market in Toyosu.

Tsukiji Market (築地市場)

Most restaurants that were in the inner market have relocated to Toyosu Market, but the outer market is still open for a sushi bowl or two. This area consists of a few very narrow lanes, lined with small restaurants and shops. Best to come for a sushi breakfast or early lunch, as most will close after this. Very traditional, if a somewhat crowded area at times! *FREE • Tsukiji station on the Metro Hibiya Line or Tsukijishijo station on the Oedo Line • Recommended rail passes: Tokyo Subway Ticket, Tokyo Metro 24-hour Ticket*

Toyosu Market (豊洲市場)

The market has been built from the ground up to accommodate tourists. While the old Tsukiji Market was too small to handle both sellers and tourists, creating a lot of friction, Toyosu Market has the size and design in place to keep both happy. Multilingual signs and explanations, as well as spacious viewing areas make this a much more comfortable experience. While this does mean some of the magic and charm of Tsukiji is gone, those who see or have seen Tsukiji will say it was really never meant for tourists. Note that there have been many delays in the opening of Toyosu Market and surrounding attractions and facilities, and some features may not be open when you plan to visit. Be sure to confirm what is open at your hostel, hotel or at a tourist information center before you go. *FREE • Opening hours and auction timings are subject to change, so confirm at your hotel/hostel a few days before (usually closed Sundays and some Wednesdays) • Shijo-mae station on the Yurikamome Line is closest. Alternatively, if you are using a subway pass, you could get off at Toyosu station on the Yurakucho Line, then walk down the road with the overhead Yurikamome Line to Shijo-mae station (about 20 minutes)*

Seafood Auctions

The markets' main attraction. See the drama, the shouting and all the big tuna sales! Visitors can watch from both a windowed, air-conditioned observation area, as well as an open observation area, where you can also experience the smells of the market.

Uogashi Yokocho

Shopping area in Building 2, full of the best tools, knives, apparel and more. This area is open to tourists, so makes for an interesting bit of window shopping, or a good spot to shop for cooking enthusiasts. You can also buy ingredients for making your own fish dish back at your hostel or hotel, or just try a few samples as you explore the complex. Additionally, there are also a few areas around the whole complex where you can grab a proper meal. Just be sure to browse around to find the best deal, as prices are seasonal and you might spot the odd special offer!

Rooftop garden

At the top of Building 2 is a spacious garden that provides awesome views over the city.

Todoroki Valley (等々力渓谷)

Todoroki Valley is a wonderful retreat from all the hustle and bustle of Tokyo. Not far from Shibuya, it offers lush forests and luminously blue waters along a short 1.2 kilometer valley. Along the way there are a few small shrines and the odd waterfall, and the whole route is almost flat, so suitable for all ages. Puzzling why this place isn't on more tourist maps! From Todoroki station, take the south exit, then walk to the right. Take a left turn down the main road and walk a little until you get to Seijo Ishii supermarket. The valley entrance is to the right of the supermarket. Walk down in a southerly direction, then when you get to the end return along the same route back to the station. *Difficulty: Easy • Walk time: 1 hour*

Budget food

There are a few cheap joints down the main shopping street. After heading out of Todoroki station (south exit) and walking to the right, take a right at the main road and walk over the tracks.

Sukiya (すき家) - Curry and gyudon eat-in and takeaway. *Meals from 360 yen • 24h*
Hotto Motto (ほっともっと) - Good bento spot, with all kinds of foods on offer. *Bento boxes from 390 yen • 7am - 11pm*

Cheap supermarkets (スーパー)
There are plenty of convenience stores around the station, in addition to the Seijo Ishii supermarket (10am-11pm) on the walk. Seijo Ishii is not the cheapest of supermarkets, but has bakery bundles and some foreign food if you are missing something back home. A cheaper option is Super Value (スーパーバリュー), which is on the street to the left after passing the above mentioned Sukiya (10am-9pm).

Free wifi locations
Currently no stable free wifi around station or near valley. Return to Shibuya if you are desperate.

How to get there and away
From Shibuya station, take the Tokyu Toyoko Line to Jiyugaoka station. From here take the Tokyu Oimachi Line to Todoroki station (16 minutes, 195 yen).

Roppongi (六本木)

Winter illuminations at Tokyo Midtown

Roppongi is known as an expensive place, but there are a few things that can be done for free. As a budget traveler, you should just do these, then get out quick!

Things to do

Winter illuminations
Roppongi has by far the most stylish, technologically sophisticated illuminations in the whole of Japan during the winter season. Tokyo Midtown has some super cool animated illuminations and displays at its Starlight Garden, while Roppongi Hills is a more low-key event, but a nice place to relax with a beer or two from the convenience store. Lines can get long at Tokyo Midtown, but the show is definitely worth it. *FREE • Tokyo Midtown: around Nov 15 – Dec 25, Roppongi Hills: around Nov 7 – Dec 25 (both 5pm-11pm)*

Louise Bourgeois' Maman (ルイーズ・ブルジョワ)

Huge bronze sculpture created by French-American artist Louise Bourgeois. It's quite a sight, with its numerous marble eggs and a 9-meter height. *FREE • Roppongi Hills*

Art galleries

There are a few galleries with free temporary exhibitions to enjoy. Pick up a copy of TimeOut Tokyo's leaflet from an information center or check their website for the latest on what's on.

Budget food

All the supermarkets are a bit pricey around here, but there are a few options for budget travelers if you don't have time to eat elsewhere.

Saizeriya (サイゼリヤ) - Light Italian dishes, such as a small pizza or pasta dish. *Pizzas from 390 yen, pasta from 399 yen • 11am-5am • Near Family Mart outside exit 2*

Kourakuen (幸楽苑) – Cheap ramen and dumplings. *Ramen from 390 yen, dumplings from 220 yen • 24h • Outside exit 4b*

Hanamaru (はなまるうどん) – Udon noodles and tempura. *From 300 yen • 10am-10pm • Outside exit 1a*

How to get there and away

Roppongi station is on the Metro **Hibiya Line** and the Toei Subway **Oedo Line**. From Shinjuku, take the Toei **Oedo Line** (216 yen), otherwise try to travel on the usually cheaper Metro. *Recommended rail passes: Tokyo Subway Ticket, Tokyo Metro 24-hour Ticket*

Tokyo Tower (東京タワー)

The iconic Tokyo Tower

While now very much overshadowed by the Skytree, and not free like the Tokyo Metropolitan Observation Decks in Shinjuku, Tokyo Tower is still very much an icon of Tokyo's post-war redevelopment. The tower still provides reasonable views over the city, with not that many of the new skyscrapers blocking your view. It's definitely a more nostalgic, less hectic experience. You can also walk up from 11am to 4pm on weekends and national holidays, if you're up for the challenge. Note that it's free on your birthday, if you happen to be traveling then! *Main Deck: Adults 900 yen, children 500 yen. Including Top Deck: Adults 2800 yen, children 1800 yen • 9am-11pm (last admission 10:30pm) • Short walk from Akabanebashi Station on the Oedo Subway Line, Kamiyacho Station on the Hibiya Metro Line and Onarimon Station on the Mita Subway Line. Also a 20-minute walk from Roppongi or Shimbashi, just aim for the tower! • Recommended rail passes: Tokyo Subway Ticket, Tokyo Metro 24-hour Ticket*

North Tokyo

Sugamo (巣鴨)

Simple shopping pleasures down Jizo Dori

Amusingly known to Tokyoites as 'Harajuku for old ladies', Sugamo is a small area in Tokyo and a popular spot for domestic tourists to visit. Elderly Japanese people love to visit to buy items colored red, which they believe will bring them luck and good health in their older age. For foreign tourists, it's a highly recommended, quirky spot if you want to see what a tourist spot is like in Japan before it's full of tourist buses and tour groups! Prices are also more reasonable than the big tourist spots in Tokyo such as Harajuku, Odaiba and Shibuya.

Things to do

Jizo Dori Shopping Street
800 meter long street, this hotspot for old ladies has plenty of bargains (old Japanese ladies love to spend the whole day looking for a good deal!) and some people like to joke that, just like the look of the area, the prices are from the 1950s as well. While not as geared up for foreign tourists as other tourist streets, this is generally a friendlier and more laid-back area. As the main market here is for the elderly, many things are rather old fashioned and not affected by modernity. Not many chains here, just family-owned, traditional businesses and the occasional free sample of tea or bean cake. *From JR Sugamo station's north exit or Metro exit A3, head north (opposite way to train bridge), Jizo Dori is the street on the left with the large gate*

Rikugien Garden (六義園)
One of our favorite Japanese gardens in Tokyo. It's got it all; cherry blossoms, autumn colors, a reasonably priced tea house, a stunning lake and lots of interesting paths to take. Come in the evening during cherry blossoms and autumn color seasons for the 'light up' events. *Adults 300 yen, children FREE • 9am-5pm (closed Dec 29 - Jan 1) • Outside Komagome station*

Sakura Onsen (サクラ 東京染井温泉)
A modern hot spring in Tokyo that uses real hot spring water, a great place for your first hot spring experience in Japan. It also includes a traditional restaurant, where you can sit on Japanese tatami mats, a relaxation zone to chill out and massage services. Plus, you can get a haircut if you really want to! Save some money by bringing your own modesty towel and bath

towel. *Adults 1296 yen, children 756 yen • 10am-11pm • Free shuttle bus every 10-15 minutes from Sugamo station (pink bus, stops near the JR south exit) or car park of swimming pool next to Sakura*

Kyu-Furukawa Gardens (旧古河庭園)

Could be described as a half English, half Japanese garden, so worth a visit if you have already been to plenty of traditional Japanese gardens. One half looks like a traditional English garden, with a manor house and roses, while the other half has a traditional Japanese pond and stone structures. Early May to early June is a great time to come for the roses and occasional free music events. *150 yen • 9am-5pm (closed Dec 29 - Jan 1) • From Komagome JR north exit or Metro exit 4, turn right (opposite side of bridge) and walk down the main road, staying on the left side. You will come to the entrance in 10 minutes*

Budget food

Jizo Dori Shopping Street

Oohashiya (大橋屋) - Traditional soba and Japanese set meals. *Soba from 750 yen • 10am-6pm*

Outside Sugamo station (north exit)

Ootoya (大戸屋) - Various Japanese set meals. *Meals from 750 yen • 11am-2am*
Hidakaya (日高屋) - Tokyo's super cheap ramen chain. Fried rice and gyoza dumplings also available. *Ramen from 390 yen • 24h*
Matsuya (松屋) - Gyudon and burger eat-in and takeaway. *Meals from 290 yen • 24h*

Cheap supermarkets (スーパー)

There is a large Seiyu (西友) near the JR north exit (24h), down the street to the left of the Jonathan's family restaurant or the dirt-cheap Hanamasa (肉のハナマサ) on Jizo Dori (24h).

Water bottle refill spots

Sakura Onsen has a water fountain in the changing rooms, so be sure to refill there.

Shopping

Apart from Jizo Dori, there are some shops on the way there, including a few 100-yen shops:
Can Do (キャンドゥ) - Head to the right from JR Sugamo station, south exit. *10am-9pm*
Silk (シルク) - Just before you enter Jizo Dori shopping street. *10am-9:30pm*

Getting around

It takes only 15 minutes or so to walk from Sugamo station to Komagome station or vice versa, to save on the train ticket. Just use a map in the station to make sure you are going in the right direction and head down the track. The tourist hotspots are short walks from either station, so the Sugamo area is a great way to spend an afternoon.

How to get there and away

From Shinjuku station, take the Yamanote Line to Sugamo station (16 mins, 165 yen). From Tokyo station, take the Yamanote Line to Sugamo station (18 mins, 165 yen). Komagome is the next station on the line. Sugamo is also on the Metro Namboku Line. *Recommended rail passes: Tokyo Subway Ticket, Tokyo Metro 24-hour Ticket, Tokyo Metropolitan District Pass*

Ikebukuro (池袋)

While not as cool and trendy as Shinjuku and Shibuya, Ikebukuro is another major hub on the circular Yamanote Line. It's a good place to do a bit of budget shopping or to pick up supplies, but the attractions here probably won't keep you for more than an afternoon or morning.

Things to do

Sunshine City (サンシャインシティ)
The largest shopping mall in Ikebukuro. Not exactly full of bargain shops, but still worth exploring, especially if looking to do some tax-free shopping. *10am-8pm • Follow street signs and maps from station. 10-minute walk*

Yamada Denki (ヤマダ電機) and Bic Camera (ビックカメラ)
These fiercely competitive electronic stores are battling it out all over Ikebukuro, meaning some good deals are to be had, especially when tax-free. *Both 10am-10pm • All over Ikebukuro, but largest ones are near the JR or Seibu east exits. Take a left, then walk towards the nearby McDonald's*

Tokyu Hands (東急ハンズ)
Large variety store, with lots of cheap gift options and tax-free shopping available. *10am-9pm • Head towards Sunshine City, Tokyu Hands is a few minutes past Uniqlo and the Sega arcade*

Nekobukuro (ねこぶくろ)
Hang out with some very adorable kittens and grab a coffee at this long-running cat café. Dress them up, take some picture and enjoy the craziness! *Adults 700 yen, children 300-500 yen • 10am-10pm • 8F of Tokyu Hands building*

Don Quijote (ドン・キホーテ)
The variety megastore chain's Ikebukuro store is packed with cheap, tax-free goods. *24h • Exits 41 and 42, or across the road from the Seibu east exit*

Muji (無印良品)
One of the larger Muji stores, this is the place to come for minimalist clothing, accessories and household goods. *10am-9pm • Head down past Don Quijote, then Lotteria, Muji is on the right*

Free sample food
The Seibu department store on the east side of the station has a large food court, with more than a few stalls offering free samples of their food, from Japanese sweets to kimchi.

Budget food

Budget restaurants
You'll never be far away from a cheap meal in Ikebukuro, but here are some favorites:
Matsuya (松屋) - Rice bowls and curry. *Gyudon bowls from 290 yen • 24h • Take a right down main road outside the east exit, walking past Don Quijote and the Can Do 100-yen shop for 5 mins*
Sushiro (スシロー) - Tasty conveyer-belt sushi. *Sushi from 120 yen • 11am-11:30pm • Continue down from Matsuya, Sushiro is just ahead at the next junction (look for the sushi poster)*
Cheap soba joints - There are a few in the station, as well as Fuji Soba (富士そば) outside the west exit, near a Matsumoto Kiyoshi (マツモトキヨシ) pharmacy.

Cheap supermarkets (スーパー)
On the east side of the station, The Garden (ザ・ガーデン) has tax-free options (10am-10pm). Considerably cheaper is the Seiyu supermarket (24h), outside Sunshine City, south entrance 3, 1F (ask at the tourist information center in the building if you get lost!).

Shopping

100-yen shops

Daiso (ダイソー) - Small but decent selection, inside Sunshine City. *10am-9pm*
Can Do (キャンドゥ) - On east side, near Don Quijote and exit 42. *10am-10pm*

Pharmacy (ドラッグストア)

The large Matsumoto Kiyoshi (マツモトキヨシ) is around the corner from Don Quijote (24h).

How to get there and away

As well as being on the JR Yamanote Line, Ikebukuro is also on the Metro Marunouchi, Yurakucho and **Fukutoshin** lines, as well as JR Saikyo and Shonan-Shinjuku lines, plus the Tobu and Seibu lines. From Shinjuku or Shibuya, either the JR Yamanote or Metro lines can be used, with JR lines being cheaper if you don't have a train pass (154 and 165 yen respectively). *Recommended rail passes: Tokyo Subway Ticket, Tokyo Metro 24-hour Ticket, Tokyo Metropolitan District Pass*

Koishikawa Korakuen (小石川後楽園)

Stunning autumn leaves at Koishikawa Korakuen

One of the largest Japanese gardens in Tokyo, Korakuen never seems to be crowded due to its huge size. The garden features elements brought over from the Ming dynasty of China, such as the 'Full Moon Bridge' and a reproduction of Seiko, a famous Chinese lake. It's also an amazing spot for autumn leaves. Also, after arriving at Iidabashi station, head up Kagurazaka (神楽坂) shopping street. You'll see lots of small paths heading off the main road, mainly to the right, that snake around some old-school dining areas. It's a pricey area for eating out but makes for a fascinating stroll. *150 yen • 9am-6pm • Korakuen station on the Metro Marunouchi and Namboku lines, Iidabashi station on the JR Chuo/Sobu lines, or Kasuga station on the Toei Oedo and Mita lines*

Cheap accommodation in Tokyo

Budget accommodation types

There are so many choices for cheap accommodation in Tokyo these days, with lots of competition to keep the prices down. The best site is Booking.com (usually free to cancel bookings), but Agoda and Airbnb also have some great deals. As the quality is very high here, you almost never hear horror stories, even at the cheapest places. Make sure you are near a train stop or an easy-to-access bus stop so that you don't waste money and time finding your place. Also consider couch surfing (https://www.couchsurfing.com/) to save on money.

Hostels and guesthouses

Hostel prices are reasonable, rooms are kept clean, bed line is properly washed and customer service is excellent. Sharing restrooms and showers is how people usually travel in Japan, so do what the locals do and save some cash on room fees.

Internet cafes

Net cafes are an even cheaper option, with prices often as low as 1000 yen. Stay in a small booth or even an open seat and chill out on the computer, or use the all-you-can-drink facilities. They can be tricky to find and confusing to use for people who don't speak Japanese, so they have been included in maps or detailed descriptions have been given in this book, plus English translations of the sleeping options. Reservations are not possible online.

Love hotels

Love hotels are a great way to stay the night in any large city in Japan, if you are with that special someone. They all have their own theme, and a variety of interesting designs. Prices start from around 6000 yen. You can either walk around and find one on the day, or choose from the increasing number that are on Booking.com or other hotel sites.

How to do a walk-in reservation at a love hotel
1) Love hotels usually have the rather Japanglish 'Rest' and 'Stay' written outside. Rest (レスト/休憩) means a stay of only a few hours, while Stay (宿泊) means to stay the night.
2) Once you are inside, there is usually an easy-to-understand picture display of rooms available. Select your room, then go and get your key. If only Japanese is written, 空室 means the room is available, 完全/満室 mean it is not.
3) You usually pay when you leave, but occasionally when you collect your key.

Capsule hotels

Capsule hotels, where guests sleep in small pods, are becoming increasingly popular with budget conscious travelers, and are a very 'only in Japan' experience. Usually costing from 2500 to 3500 yen, depending on spa facilities and location, they offer a great way to stay the night in the city center. While some are men-only, many offer women-only floors. Note that some capsule hotels are usually just for the night, and will not allow you to keep your luggage there during the day. You can put your bags in a locker at a nearby station if that is the case.

Overnight spas

Some hot springs or spas allow people to spend a little extra to stay the night. Guests usually sleep in lazyboy chairs or on tatami mats, with pillows and blankets provided. Great way to save on room costs, plus people are usually so sleepy after a long dip in the hot spring baths, that it doesn't matter if the sleeping arrangements are rather basic.

Recommended budget accommodation in Tokyo

Hostels and guest houses

Tokyo Guest House Ouji Music Lounge (東京ゲストハウス王子ミュージックラウンジ)
Super friendly staff, with clean and spacious dorms. Occasionally has free breakfast offers, as well as live music events. Could not come more highly recommended. *Dorms from 2750 yen • Near Oji station, a short ride from Ueno •* http://oji-music-lounge.tokyo/

Tokyo Guest House Itabashi-juku (東京ゲストハウス 板橋宿)
Quiet dorms with a large lounge and basic kitchen facilities. Lots of cheap restaurants and supermarkets around it too. *Dorms from 2000 yen • Naka-Itabashi station, 10 mins from Ikebukuro •* http://guesthousejapan.tokyo/en/

Khaosan Hostels (カオサン)
This well-known guesthouse chain has a variety of cheap and clean guesthouses in central locations. They all have their own unique theme, so they are a bit nicer to stay at than a dull YHA hostel. *Dorms from 2200 yen, private rooms from 3400 yen •* http://khaosan-tokyo.com/en/

Anne Hostel Asakusabashi (浅草橋旅荘 庵)
Free breakfast is provided at this friendly hostel. Highly recommended by many travelers. *Dorms from 2800 yen, private rooms from 3400 yen • Near Ueno and Akihabara*

Tatami Guesthouse (畳ゲストハウス)
A bit further away than most others, but we have stayed here and would highly recommend the place. It's very cheap, is in a quiet area and there are lots of people around to help you in your travels (one Japanese guy took us on a free tour of an animation museum!). *Private rooms from 2100 yen • Hibarigaoka station •* http://www.tatami-guesthouse.com/

GrapeHouse Koenji (female only) (ゲストハウス グレープハウス高円寺)
This ladies-only hostel has a great reputation and gets full up easily, so try to book as early as possible. Friendly staff can help you to get around. *Dorms from 3500 • Koenji station •* http://grapehouse.jp/en/

Shrek Watta House
A nice guesthouse, we have stayed here several times. Has both western and Japanese style tatami mat rooms. Run by a nice old man, this place has a nice open kitchen with loads of free travel resources. *Private rooms from 2150 yen • Musashi-Seki station, near Shinjuku station •* http://www.shrek-watta-house.com/index.html

Tokyo Central Youth Hostel (東京セントラルユースホステル)
A clean, reasonably priced hostel (especially if you are a Hostelling International Member) right bang in the center of Tokyo. Great for large groups or families. *Dorms from 3360 yen • Above Iidabashi station (JR and Metro lines) •* http://www.jyh.gr.jp/tcyh/e/top.html

For the family

While it can sometimes be tricky for families to find a place, with too many hotel rooms in double or twin configurations, more options are slowly becoming available. These days many locals are renting out their apartments on Airbnb and Booking.com, so these sites are great options for families. Just be prepared for smaller rooms than you would get in other countries, and don't expect to get a swimming pool without spending your whole holiday budget. But as long as your place is near a train station, traveling with kids here is very easy. Also remember that Tokyo is a safe society with many kid friendly spots, so perfect for the family. For families, the above Shrek Watta House and Tokyo Central Youth Hostel would be great choices.

Overnight Spas (super sentos)

Oedo-Onsen Monogatari Hot Spring (大江戸温泉物語)

It's also possible to stay the night here in Odaiba's huge onsen, where you can sleep in the tatami rooms or in the lazyboy chairs. *2160 yen extra to stay overnight • Near Telecom Center Station in Odaiba*

LaQua (スパ ラクーア)

A huge hot spring, taking water from 1700 meters below Tokyo. There are plenty of areas to sleep for the night. *Entrance fee: Adults 2850 yen, children 2052 yen, 1944 yen extra to stay overnight • Near Korakuen station*

Capsule hotels

Akihabara

Capsule Value Kanda (men only)

You will soon realize why they have a 91% rating. Really helpful staff, cheap bike rental and inexpensive rooms. *Capsules from 2400 yen • From Kanda station, take the south exit, walk down the track and take left turn at 2nd road under track •* http://capsuleinn.com/kanda/en/

First Cabin Akihabara

More upmarket than Capsule Value, with spacious capsules and hotel like facilities. *Capsule from 3700 yen • From Metro Hibiya exit 4, 1 min down 2nd road parallel to river*

Asakusa

Capsule Hotel Asakusa River Side

A very cheap capsule hotel with English support, right next to Asakusa station. *Capsules from 2000 yen • Opposite exit A5*

Shibuya

Capsule Hotel Shibuya (Men only) (カプセルホテル渋谷)

Cheap capsule hotel right in the center of Shibuya. *Capsules from 3500 yen • West side of station*

Shinjuku

Hatagoya (カプセルホテルはたごや)

Looks more like a new ryokan (Japanese hotel) from the outside, this new capsule hotel is modern, clean and has free soap and shampoo in the showers. *Capsules from 3200 yen •* http://hatago-ya.com/

nine hours Shinjuku-North (ナインアワーズ 北新宿)

Trustworthy capsule hotel chain. Great English-language support at the 24h front desk. *Capsules from 3000 yen •* https://ninehours.co.jp/

Ikebukuro

Book and Bed Tokyo

You may have seen this place on the blogosphere, and there's a good reason why. Book and Bed is essentially a capsule hotel inside a library. It's a very unique, 'only in Japan' experience. Also, as expected of a library, it's super quiet. *Dorms from 3800 yen • Near Ikebukuro, Shinjuku or Asakusa stations •* http://bookandbedtokyo.com/

Love hotels (adults only)

Kabukicho in Shinjuku is a heartland for love hotels, so head to the northern area if you don't have a reservation and want to see what's available. Also great is Love Hotel Hill (ラブホテル坂) in Shibuya, which has a bewildering range. Take your time to compare prices and facilities available. The ones available to reserve online are often two or three times as expensive as just turning up, but try Booking.com if you want that peace of mind. *'Rest' (2-4 hours) from 2000 yen, 'Stay' (overnight) from 6000 yen*

Internet cafes

Akihabara

You are really spoilt for choice here, so here are just a few safe bets.

Monkey Net (もんきーねっと)

Good choice of free services, plus cool extras like all-you-can eat ice cream. *Night pack (ナイトパック) available from 5pm: 6 hours (6 時間ナイトパック) from 980 yen, 9 hours (9 時間ナイトパック) from 1278 yen • West side of station*

Ai Cafe Akiba Place (アイ・カフェ)

Huge choice of comics, drinks and ice cream. Also has free food! Rice bowls, toast and curry on the house. Note the cheapest prices are for cafeteria seats. *Night pack (ナイトパック) available from 6pm: 6 hours (6 時間ナイトパック) from 1060 yen, 9 hours (9 時間ナイトパック) from 1660 yen • Head up Chuo Dori and take first left after Don Quijote*

Shibuya

Head down Inokashira Dori, parallel to Center Gai for a good selection of net cafes:

Bagus (バグース)

Large choice of comics, clean showers and good selection of free drinks. *Night pack (ナイトパック) available from 9pm: 6 hours (6 時間ナイトパック) from 1150 yen. 9 hours (9 時間ナイトパック) from 1800 yen*

Manbo (マンボー)

Japan's largest chain. Free showers, comics and drinks. *Night pack (ナイトパック) available from 7pm: 6 hours (6 時間ナイトパック) from 1300 yen*

Media Cafe Popeye (メディアカフェポパイ)

Modern net cafe with free drinks, showers and printing services. *Night pack (ナイトパック) available from 6pm: 6 hours (6 時間ナイトパック) from 950 yen. 12 hours (12 時間ナイトパック) from 1380 yen*

Shinjuku

Manbo (マンボー)

This net cafe chain has several chains around the station, so if this branch is full, ask for the others. Free showers, comics and drinks. *Night pack (ナイトパック) available from 7pm: 6 hours (6 時間ナイトパック) from 1500 yen • Head down Yasukuni Dori, passing east side Yamada Denki LABI. Manbo is just after the Family Mart, on the right*

Bagus (バグース)

Similar to Manbo, but generally quieter and with not so bright lights, so it's easier to sleep. Also has a ladies-only section. *Night pack (ナイトパック) available from 7pm: 6 hours (6 時間ナイトパック) from 1150 yen. 9 hours (9 時間ナイトパック) from 1430 yen • Next block on from above Manbo*

Side trips from Tokyo

Tokyo is situated in Kanto, the most built-up and prosperous of all the prefectures in Japan. The prefecture has a great transportation network, with many spots not far away, making Tokyo a perfect base from which to do some side trips on a budget. The highlight is of course Mount Fuji, a great challenge that any traveler should tick off their bucket list. Other highlights include the relaxing hot spring town of Hakone, the spiritual temple town of Nikko and Tokyo's little brother city of Yokohama. The multiple discount transportation passes are perfect for budget travelers.

Discount passes

JR Tokyo Wide Pass
Most of the spots in this chapter have discount transportation passes of their own, but if you want to do many of them in a short amount of time, the JR Tokyo Wide Pass may be worth a look. It allows unlimited use of JR trains (and a few partner lines) in the Kanto prefecture for three consecutive days, including use of Shinkansen and limited express trains. The pass is available from a JR Travel Service Center in any major station in Tokyo or Yokohama, plus Narita and Haneda airports. Note the pass is for those with tourist visas only.

The JR Tokyo Wide Pass covers most of the places in this chapter. It provides access to Kamakura, Kawagoe, Nikko, Mitake, Takao and Yokohama. It would be possible to visit one of these each day, so have a look and see which take your fancy. The pass does not include the unlimited use of local transportation in these areas, which the individual passes for tourist areas do. The following spots require a short journey on a train line or bus not covered by the pass: Mount Oyama (180 yen extra from Atsugi station), Hakone (310 yen extra from Odawara station) and Mount Fuji (2100 yen extra from Kawaguchiko). In conclusion, if you are in a rush and want to really pack in lots in those three days, this pass is worth it, but otherwise it's probably easier and cheaper to get each area's own discount pass, or individual cheap local or express train tickets. *Adults 10000 yen, children 5000 yen*

Greater Tokyo Pass
A new pass introduced for the use of private train lines and buses in and around Kanto. Allowing three days of unlimited travel, it can be used with dozens of private operators and includes the use of the subways in Tokyo (but not the use of any JR lines). It's therefore worth it, and you'll save a bit, if you can get to all your desired destinations on non-JR lines, so check the information for how to get to each place in the relevant chapter. Note the service area doesn't reach Fuji or Hakone. Available to buy at major private train or subway stations, or at one of the airports. *Adults 7200 yen, children 3600 yen* • https://greater-tokyo-pass.jp/

Yokohama (横浜)

Actually the second largest city in Japan and only 30 minutes from Tokyo, Yokohama has long since become part of the grand metropolis. What sets this city apart is its port and the rich history of foreign culture and trade. Makes for a fun day trip, especially if you have already done lots of Tokyo before. When you arrive, head to the nearest tourist information center and pick up one of their large maps. If you are using the **Minato Mirai Line**, our recommended spots are shown, but it also features seasonal walking routes.

European style buildings and gardens in Motomachi

Discount pass: Minato Mirai Line One Day Pass

The best way to get to and around Yokohama. Minato Mirai Line One Day Pass allows visitors to use the **Minato Mirai Line** an unlimited amount of times in Yokohama, plus use of a return ticket from Shibuya in Tokyo on the Tokyu Line if required. If you don't want to walk around all day (distances can be large here) and want to save time by using the trains, this is a great pass. If you really love walking a lot, you could just walk around Yokohama with a map from the tourist information center in the station. Buy it from the Tokyu ticket offices. *From Tokyo: Adults 840 yen, Children 420 yen. From Yokohama station: Adults 460 yen, Children 230 yen*

A little bit of history

Way back in 1859, Yokohama was a small village of 600 when it opened its first port. The city from then on started to blossom as a modern trading post, in particular in the export of Japanese tea and silk. The Great Kanto Earthquake destroyed much of Yokohama in 1923, but it was not long before the city returned to its former glory. Devastation to the city came again in WWII and the city was initially slow to redevelop. Thankfully Japan's economic boom came along in the 80s and 90s, triggering rapid growth and leading to a very modern, clean city.

Things to do

Minato Mirai 21 District

The following are all near Minato Mirai station on the **Minato Mirai Line**:

Cupnoodles Museum (カップヌードルミュージアム)

A strange but wonderful museum. From the first chicken noodles, to the hundreds of current variations, this museum is all about instant noodles and their inventor, Momofuku Ando. There is also a world noodle food court, strange noodle-based art and a noodle kitchen to make your own custom noodles. A real 'only in Japan' experience, and fun for all the family. *Adults 500 yen, Children FREE • 10am-6pm (closed New Year holidays and Tuesdays. When Tuesday is a holiday, closed the following day)*

Yokohama Cosmo World (コスモワールド)
Much cheaper, and more nostalgic, than going to Disney World. Visitors can buy individual ride tickets to keep costs down, with a water ride, roller coaster, Ferris wheel and more. *FREE entry (rides 300-700 yen) • Weekdays 11am-9pm, weekends 11am-10pm (closed Thursdays)*

Yokohama Red Brick Warehouses (横浜赤レンガ倉庫)
Back in the 1920s, these mega brick warehouses were the Customs Inspection House for boats coming into the harbor. It has since been converted into a hip area for all to enjoy. Best for budget travelers are the frequent festivals, usually on weekends, such as October Beer Fest in autumn, ice skating in the winter and free concerts in the summer. *FREE • 10am-7pm*

Yokohama Museum of Art (横浜美術館)
A wide, but manageable collection of art. The main sections have late 19th century works from artists such as Milo, Picasso and Dali, while others feature artists with ties to Yokohama. Features excellent English explanations and children's workshops, plus occasionally has free access days. *Adults 500 yen, high school children and above 300 yen, elementary and under 100 yen • 10am-6pm (closed New Year holidays and Thursdays)*

Yokohama Landmark Tower (ランドマークタワー)
Get a view 273 meters above Yokohama, after enjoying a 750 meters per minute elevator. Not essential, but most travelers head up on clear days as the tower also provides stunning views over to Tokyo. *Adults 1000 yen, children 200-800 yen • 10am-9pm*

Yamashita
Head to Nihon-Odori station on the Minato Mirai Line to visit Yokohama's famous port area:

Yamashita Park (山下公園)
Yokohama's main park and a good spot to start your adventures. In the summer there are usually events here every week.

Osanbashi Yokohama International Passenger Terminal (大さん橋)
Very funky design for this ultramodern passenger terminal. Made of strips of wood, the winding structure is very unique piece of abstract architecture. Well worth a relaxing stroll, especially with a beer at night, watching over the city lights.

Chinatown (中華街)
Japan's biggest Chinatown, dwarfing most others. As you walk around, there will be more than a few sellers offering free samples of Chinese snacks or drinks, but maybe not as many bargains as you may be expecting. Budget travelers should completely avoid going to the restaurants on the main street as they have a bad reputation for charging tourist prices, but some of the side streets can be more reasonable.

Motomachi (元町)
A nice area featuring lots of registered historical buildings, parks and churches. Feels like a mix between Japan and Europe. Some of the buildings charge a small fee for entrance, but there are plenty of free options, so no need to pay unless you are particularly into the history and architecture of Yokohama. There are more than a dozen such buildings and sites to see, but here are the best spots to check out:

Ehrisman Residence
Finished in 1926 as the residence of Fritz Ehrismann, a prominent exporter and importer of sought-after products like silk. His vast wealth allowed him to commission Antonin Raymond to design the building, who was considered to be a master of modern architecture at the time. *FREE • 9:30am-5pm (6pm in summer) (closed New Year holidays)*

Berrick Hall

The local residence of British trading merchant B.R. Berrick, this building was constructed in 1930. It later served as the dormitory for an international school, but since 2000 has been open to the general public. Once you get here, you will soon realize why it is such an in-demand wedding venue, with its picturesque grounds and classic interior. *FREE • 9:30am-5pm (6pm in summer) (closed New Year holidays)*

Bluff No. 234

Prettily lit up in the evening, this building dates back to 1927, when it was an apartment for the new foreigners entering via Yokohama Bay. Detailed panels help to enlighten guests about the history of the area. *FREE • 9:30am-5pm (6pm in summer) (closed New Year holidays)*

Shin-Yokohama Ramen Museum

We sure did stuff ourselves here. Calling itself a "ramen amusement park", this museum is a fantastic way to try various types of Japanese noodles. Portions can be small, but the usually lower prices should allow you to try out a few, including giving the crazier varieties a try. *Adults 310 yen, children 100 yen, under 6 FREE • 11am-11pm • Just north of Shin-Yokohama station*

Volunteer guides and tours

Kanagawa Good Will Guide Club - http://volunteerguide-ksgg.jp/
Offers a guided tour along Yokohama waterfront, so includes all the highlights. Try to book more than two weeks in advance.

Budget food

Yokohama is quite spread out, so if you do come across somewhere cheap, and it's around time to eat, grab the chance and head inside.

Yokohama World Porters

There are a few cheap spots in Yokohama World Porters shopping mall, opposite the Cup Noodle Museum in Minato Mirai:

Saizeriya (サイゼリヤ) - Light Italian dishes, such as a small pizza or pasta dish. *Pizzas from 390 yen, pasta from 399 yen • 10am-11pm*

Steak Mountain (鉄板ステーキチャーハン) - Steaks on fried rice. *Plates from 790 yen • 10:30am-9pm*

Landmark Tower

There is a large selection in Landmark Tower, as well as in the connected Queen's Square. Most are quite expensive, but there are a few good budget options:

Tsukemen Tetsu (つけめん TETSU) - Famous dipping noodles shop, with some super tasty soup. *Meals from 780 yen • 11am-11pm*

Vie De France (ヴィ・ド・フランス) - Reasonably cheap bakery and cafe, which often cuts prices in the evening. *Breads from 150 yen • 7:30am-9pm*

Cheap supermarkets (スーパー)

If you in Yokohama station, the best is Tokyu Store (東急ストア) on the north side of the building (10am-10pm). Near Chinatown, outside Motomachi-Chukagai station is Maruetsu Petit (マルエツ プチ), a large 24-hour supermarket (opposite exit 2). There are also numerous small supermarkets around.

Water bottle refill spots

Yamashita Koen has some water fountains, as does Motomachi Koen (元町公園) in the Motomachi area and the park on the coast in Minato Mirai.

Shopping

100-yen shops

Daiso (ダイソー) - Inside 'Mark Is' shopping mall (マークイズみなとみらい), next to Minato Mirai station (10am-8pm). There is also one outside Yokohama station, west exit, opposite Yodobashi Camera, plus on Chukagai Odori (main street in Chinatown).

Seria (セリア) - In World Portal (ワールドポーターズ), the shopping mall opposite Cosmo World in Minato Mirai. *10:30am-9pm*

Pharmacy (ドラッグストア)

Matsumoto Kiyoshi (マツモトキヨシ) has a store inside Yokohama station (10am-10pm).

Recommended cheap accommodation

Hostels and guest houses

Hayashi Kaikan (Yokohama Hostel Village)

Probably the cheapest place to stay in Yokohama. Hardly the Ritz, but you can't argue with these prices! Not totally central, but a short walk from all the action. *Dorms from 2400 yen* • http://yokohama.hostelvillage.com/en/

Hostel Zen

Another well-known hostel, which is smaller than others and seems to have a nice, friendly atmosphere. Various plans and rooms types available. *Dorms from 2800 yen*

Capsule hotels and overnight spas

Sky Spa Yokohama (スカイスパ横浜)

Quite a selection of baths they have here! Modern, centrally located and with clean capsules to sleep in. *Overnight passes from 4700 yen* • *In Marui City, to east side of Yokohama station*

Spa & Capsule Hotel Grand Park-Inn (スパ&カプセルホテル グランパーク・イン)

More of a standard capsule hotel than the others, so prices are a little lower, though there are some spa facilities. In a slightly seedy area, but not in any way too much so. *Capsules from 3500 yen* • *West side of Yokohama station, near subway exit 9. Walk to right, then take first right after a bit, then left and down*

Manyo Club (横浜みなとみらい 万葉倶楽部)

Super fun, or relaxing, way to spend your evening, night and morning. Large variety of baths, including outside ones overlooking Tokyo Bay, game arcades, stone relaxation rooms and more. Overnighters can catch 40 winks in the lazyboy chairs, or in the tatami rooms. *Overnight passes from 4500 yen* • http://www.manyo.co.jp/mm21/eng/

Internet cafes (ネットカフェ)

The biggest collection of net cafes is on the west side of Yokohama station. It's fun to have a look around, but go to these safe bets if you are new to net cafes:

Manbo (マンボー)

Free showers, comics and drinks. They also have other branches nearby, so ask if they are full. *8 hours (8 時間ナイトパック) from 1350 yen* • *Bit tricky to get to, so use wifi in Yokohama station. Near subway exit 9*

Hanatato (花太郎)

Some amazing deals, especially on weekdays. Showers included, plus the usual free drinks. You can leave and come back on night packages. *13 hours night package (ナイトパック) from 2100 yen* • *Also tricky to get to, so use wifi in Yokohama station. Near subway exit 9*

How to get there and away

If on the west wide of Tokyo, it's usually cheapest to go via Shibuya. From Shibuya station, take the Tokyu **Toyoko Line** to Yokohama station (30 mins, 267 yen or covered with the Minato Mirai Line One Day Pass). From Tokyo station on the east side of Tokyo, take the JR **Tokaido Line** to Yokohama station (30 mins, 464 yen). *Recommended Kanto rail passes: JR Tokyo Wide Pass, Greater Tokyo Pass*

Tourist information (観光案内所)

Inside Yokohama station's central passage (9am-7pm).

Mount Fuji (富士山)

Japan's most iconic mountain, now a UNESCO World Heritage site, should be on the top of most travelers' plans for a trip to the Land of the Rising Sun. The highest mountain in Japan at 3,776 meters, its grand size straddles over various prefectures. It is also one of Japan's "Three Holy Mountains" and has been the site of pilgrimage to Japanese people for centuries. In Shinto mythology, the god Kuninotokotachi is believed to reside at the top. For us mere mortals, the view from the top of Mount Fuji has to be seen to be believed. While it can get very busy, this will probably be your most memorable experience in Japan and it's surprisingly cheap to visit. Just be sure to bring a warm coat for the chilly summit!

Yoshida Trail

Most budget travelers coming from Tokyo should take this, as getting there is easiest. While it can be steep and challenging, even to the fairly fit, it's a great reward to get to the views at the top. *Difficulty: Medium • Hike time: 9-10 hours return • Hiking season: Around July 1 to Sept 10*

Fujinomiya Trail

The second most popular trail, this is definitely worth considering if you have a Japan Rail Pass. The starting point is also the highest of all the trails, so the trip to the top is shortest, if a little steep at times. Note that hikers will not see the sunrise before reaching the summit on this trail. *Difficulty: Medium • Hike time: 6-9 hours return • Hiking season: Around July 10 to Sept 10*

Subashiri Trail

Less crowded than the other two for most of the trail (it eventually meets up with the Yoshida trail), the Subashiri trail is also less developed. Facilities are therefore not as good as the others, but if you are willing to sacrifice this for a quieter experience, this trail may be worth the effort. *Difficulty: Medium • Hike time: 8-12 hours return • Hiking season: Around July 10 to Sept 10*

When to come

The best time to arrive is in the evening. If you start heading up by 8-10pm, by the time you get to the top you should have perfect timing to watch the spectacular sunrise. It's truly one of the most amazing sights you will ever see, and perfectly safe to do. Plus walking up overnight saves on having to book a room somewhere. Another tip is to come on the weekdays and outside holidays, to avoid large families with children.

Budget food

While there are some souvenir shops and restaurants around the bus stops, the prices are not so good and choice is limited for food to actually take up. Surprisingly, there are some noodle stalls up the mountain, but prices are really high and these stalls should be avoided unless you are starving. Go to a supermarket the night before and get yourself plenty of drinks and food for the long hike.

Water bottle refill spots

There are no free water fountains as you head up, and the price of drinks (yes, there is a vending machine at the top!) get very expensive, so by the time you get to the shop at the summit they are about four times what you would normally pay.

Pharmacy (ドラッグストア)

The shops at the bases have some basics, but bring any essential medicine.

Recommended cheap accommodation

There are several mountain huts on the way up, all of which charge to stay. Prices are rather high for a basic hut experience, but if you feel 8-10 hours walking all in one go is too much for you, they are worth it. Fujisan Mountain Guides can also provide a booking service in English (1000 yen), if you are having trouble finding a bed.

Yoshida Trail

These two have English websites, but try to reserve as soon as possible to hold your spot.

Kamaiwa-kan (鎌岩館)
Brand new, stylish building about halfway up, so a perfect spot to have a sleep before continuing up. Can also provide basic food like curry or burgers. *Bed from 6000 yen with no meals on weekdays, 7800 yen on weekends (with two meals) •* http://kamaiwakan.jpn.org/ *(online discounts sometimes available)*

Haku-un-so (白雲荘)
Very near to the summit, this hut will break your journey in half. With more than 300 beds, this place can get packed, but the prices are pretty good for the location. Food can also be provided, and there is a small shop if you have forgotten anything. *Bed from 5800 yen with no meals •* http://fujisan-hakuun.com/en/reservation/

Fujinomiya Trail

Fuji Fujinomiya Climbing Association (富士山表富士宮口登山組合)

These guys help run several mountain huts, each spaced out along the trail. While some only take reservations via telephone, others allow bookings via email or online. Just check each hut's page via http://www.fuji-tozan.com/04_lodge.html. If you cannot read Japanese, use Google Translate. *Bed from 5500 yen with no meals (plus 1000 yen on Saturday)*

Chojo Fujikan (頂上富士館)

Especially recommended is this hut right at the top, so essentially half way along your hiking experience. Friendly staff and some wholesome food. Bookings at this one can also be made online. *Bed from 5500 yen with no meals* • http://fujisanchou.com/guide-for-english/

Subashiri Trail

There are nine huts as you go up and one on the descent.

Oyama-Town Sightseeing Near Fuji

This excellent site has all the mountain huts available on the trail. The 5th station ones are at the bottom, while the 8th is near the top. Click on the mountain hut website links to see more info. You can then book via email or web form (with the help of Google Translate!). All the mountain huts on this trail offer basic facilities, but that should be all you need if you bring some food and drinks with you. *Beds from 4000 yen with no meals* • http://www.fuji-oyama.jp/kankoubunka_fuji_yamagoya.html

How to get there and away

Yoshida Trail

From Tokyo, the cheapest and fastest way is to get a highway bus from Shinjuku Bus Terminal in Shinjuku, with Keio Bus (operated May through October). You must reserve in advance at the terminal or on the Keio Bus website. The tickets cost 2700 yen (discounts may be given if you book more than a month ahead, children half price). From Kawaguchiko station in Fuji Five Lakes, Keio Bus also run regular services (2100 yen for round trip, children half price). You could use this bus if traveling on a JR Tokyo Wide Pass or national Japan Rail Pass.

Fujinomiya Trail

The trail can be accessed via buses from Shin-Fuji from mid-July to the end of August. This station is on the Tokaido Shinkansen Line which heads from Tokyo down to Osaka and Kyoto, so budget travelers should only use this trail if they have a Japan Rail Pass. Buses depart about every hour from outside the station until 5pm (2 hours, round trip: adults 3100 yen, children 1550 yen; one way: adults 2390 yen, children 1190 yen). Reservations not required.

Subashiri Trail

First, you need to make your way to Gotemba station. From Tokyo station, take the JR Tokaido Line to Kozu, then the JR **Gotemba Line** to Gotemba (2 hours, 1940 yen). Next, there are hourly buses until 6:25pm that can take you to the trail start (1 hour, round trip: adults 2600 yen, children 1030 yen; one way: adults 1540 yen, children 770 yen). No reservations required.

Tourist information (観光案内所)

For the Yoshida trail, there is one near the final bus stop (9am-4:30pm, until 8pm July 1 - Sept 11). There is also one near Shin-Fuji station (8:45am-5:30pm) for the Fujinomiya trail.

Nikko (日光)

Toshogu Shrine, Nikko

Probably the most impressive side trip from Tokyo, Nikko is one of Japan's many UNESCO World Heritage sites. It's a town full of temples, shrines, waterfall and lakes. The World Heritage area includes two shrines and a temple, but there are lots of other cheap touristy things to do as well. There are also a few non-traditional, crazy experiences, such as the Edo inspired theme park and a miniatures theme park. Nikko also has excellent English signage.

Discount passes: Tobu Nikko Passes

From Asakusa in Tokyo, Tobu Railways has two kinds of passes. They are an obvious pick for budget travelers, as there is not much else in the area apart from the locations on the passes, and everything can be comfortably done in the time allowed. You can buy them at the Tobu Sightseeing Service Center in Tobu Asakusa station. The passes include unlimited use of buses (and trains if applicable) to the main spots. Because some of the areas in Nikko are quite spaced out, you will need to use the bus at least a few times. You'll save a lot!

Discounts included
The passes give 20% off limited express tickets (only saves 30 minutes or so, so not essential), 5% off at some shops in Asakusa, 10% off for purchases over 1000 yen at some shops in Nikko and discounts to more than a dozen tourist spots in Nikko. Look for the logos in the pass for where you can get money off.

Nikko Pass - world heritage area
This pass is the best way to visit Nikko and Kinugawa Onsen for most budget travelers. The two days provide plenty of time to see all the main shrines and temples in this UNESCO World Heritage site area. It includes a round ticket from Tokyo. Note that the service area does not extend outside the main area, such as to Lake Chuzenji. *Adults 2000 yen, children 600 yen*

Nikko Pass – all areas

Four days are included on this pass, as well as expanded use of the bus network beyond the main tourist spots, including to the onsen towns in the north and to Edo Wonderland. *April-November: Adults 4520 yen, children 1150 yen. December-March: Adults 4150 yen, children 2070 yen*

Things to do

Toshogu Shrine (日光東照宮)

The most well-known World Heritage shrine in Nikko, and recently renovated. It enshrines the first Shogun of the Edo Shogunate, Tokugawa Ieyasu. This temple complex leads into the forested mountain, and will blow you away with its stunning buildings and national treasures (8 national treasures and 34 important cultural properties in total). Head up the stone stairs at the back for a cool walk up to another shrine up the small mountain. *Adults 800, children 600 yen • 8am-5pm (8am-4pm in the winter) • 'Nishi-sando' bus stop*

Shinkyo Bridge (神橋)

Beautiful wooden Japanese red bridge, at the entrance to the Nikko mountains. The myth goes that when a head priest, named Shodo Shonin, was not able to cross the Daiyagawa River he was helped by the gods. Two snakes appeared and constructed the bridge so he could cross. *FREE • 'Shinkyo' bus stop, then follow signs. Walkable from nearby shrines*

Rinno-ji Temple (日光山輪王寺)

A large temple surrounded by huge trees, this is one of the largest wooden structures in the area. Founded more than 1000 years ago, the complex features a grand hall with statues of various gods, a treasure house exhibiting statues of Buddha and other important cultural properties. Also as a Japanese garden called Shoyoen. *Adults 1000 yen, children 600 yen • 8am-5pm (8am-4pm in the winter) • 'Nishi-sando' bus stop*

Futarasan Temple (二荒山神社)

A quiet temple within the forests of Nikko, and a site for followers to worship nearby Mount Futarasan. It's famous for offering good luck to those who pray in the forest-enclosed complex, for important life changes such as pregnancy or marriage. A soon as you arrive you will realize why Nikko is a World Heritage site. *200 yen • 8am-5pm (8am-4pm in the winter) • 'Nishi-sando' bus stop, or walk from Shinkyo bridge*

Taiyuin Temple (大猷院)

A big complex of temple buildings in the forested mountains, this is the mausoleum of Tokugawa Iemitsu. It was constructed to face Toshogu Shrine, but in a subtle way, so as to not overshadow it. The main hall and front shrines are registered as national treasures, but explore around as there are some excellent examples of ancient craftsmanship in the various structures. *550 yen • 8am-6pm • 'Nishi-sando' bus stop, or walk from Shinkyo bridge*

Kegon Waterfall (華厳の滝)

A tall waterfall not far from the center of Nikko, and the most popular. The water from Lake Chuzenji falls almost 100 meters, and the viewing platforms give a good view from below. Great any time of the year. *550 yen • 8am-5pm (9am-4:30pm in the winter) • 'Chuzenji-onsen' bus stop*

Lake Chuzenji (中禅寺湖)

Created more than 20,000 years ago when Mount Nantai erupted. This 11.62 km squared lake was once surrounded by foreign embassies and estates in the Meiji period, so was known for its beauty for many years before tourists arrived. Have a walk around the lake and take some awesome photos to share with your friends (just remember to mention @SuperCheapJapan!). *FREE • 'Tachikikannon-iriguchi' bus stop or short walk from Kegon Waterfall*

Ryuzu Waterfall (竜頭ノ滝)

On the north-west of Lake Chuzenji is this nice waterfall and park, a quieter spot than Kegon Waterfall. If you have time, walk up to Lake Yunoko and Yudaki Falls. *FREE • 'Akanuma' bus stop*

Tobu World Square (東武ワールドスクウェア)

A lighthearted, and up-to-date outdoor museum with miniature reproductions of more than 100 famous buildings and structures from across the world. Appropriately for Nikko, it includes 45 World Heritage sites at a 1/25 scale. *2800 yen (see website to check for 500 yen discount coupon) • 8am-5pm (8am-4pm in the winter) • Get bus from Kinugawa-onsen station, near to Nikko •* https://www.tobuws.co.jp/en/

Edo Wonderland Nikko Edomura (日光江戸村)

Experience the old city of Edo (former name of Tokyo), at this faithful, but fun reproduction. The houses, downtown area and ninja village are great if you need a break away from all the temples. Also interesting to see the 'locals' walking around, doing their daily tasks and jobs. *One Day Pass: adults 4700 yen, children 2400 yen. Afternoon Pass (from 2pm, or 1pm in winter): adults 4100 yen, children 2100 yen • 9am-5pm (9:30am-4pm in the winter) • Get bus from Kinugawa-onsen station, nearby Nikko •* http://edowonderland.net/en/

Hike for free

There are plenty of hikes that start from near the town center or are a short distance from a bus stop, but there are a few real highlights. More routes can be found in the tourist information centers, where free hiking and walking maps are available.

Mount Nakimushi

Famous mountain, which can be accessed just south of the train stations. Small waterfalls, pristine forest and the religious ornaments along the way make it an enjoyable hike. *Difficulty: Medium • Hike time: 4-5 hours*

Lake Chuzenji

A variety of routes are available, but the South-Bank Course (starting from near Kegon Waterfall) is a nice balance of lake and hills. *Difficulty: Easy • Hike time: 4-5 hours*

Lake Yunoko

This smaller lake is a perfect quick and easy hike, which offers views of Yudaki Falls and the nearby Onsen Shrine. Access from Yudaki Falls bus stop. *Difficulty: Easy • Hike time: 1 hour*

Volunteer guides and tours

Utsunomiya SGG Club - http://www016.upp.so-net.ne.jp/usgg/
Provides guides for Nikko from the nearby city of Utsunomiya. This does mean you have to pay for them to come to Nikko, but it's still a good deal if you want an in-depth experience. Apply at least two weeks in advance.

Budget food

Few budget chain restaurants in the area, presumably to keep the place more authentic. Head north up Nihon Romantic Highway from Nikko station for a selection of restaurants, but they are quite spaced out. There are some tonkatsu (deep fried cutlet) and ramen joints up here, but good prices may be hard (and time consuming) to find. If you are stuck around the station, head to the supermarket for a large choice of cheap takeouts and microwavable items.

Cheap supermarkets (スーパー)

Lion Dor (リオン・ドール) is five-minute walk from Tobu Nikko station. Head out and then walk down the road with the post office on the right (9am-9pm).

Water bottle refill spots

Bring a large bottle of water from your hostel/hotel, just in case you can't or don't go to a restaurant with some way to refill.

Shopping

100-yen shops

meets (ミーツ) - Down the river to the north side of the station. *9am-9pm*

Pharmacy (ドラッグ ストア)

Welcia (ウエルシア) - From the JR Nikko station, head down the road to the left of Nikko Station Hotel Classic, then take a left at the second traffic lights and walk a few minutes. *9am-9pm*

Recommended cheap accommodation

Hostels and guest houses

Minsyuku Rindo-no-ie

Very cheap hostel with Japanese tatami floors and friendly customer service. Also has a large bath. *Dorms from 3500* • http://outdoor.geocities.jp/rindoutyan/

Nikko Suginamiki Youth Hostel

Great if you are a Youth Hostel member, this place is also good for small groups. *Dorms from 3360 yen* • http://www.jyh.or.jp/e/i.php?jyhno=2208

Nikko Guesthouse Sumica

Traditional rooms with Japanese tatami mats and a really friendly atmosphere. Right next to the station, yet still some of the cheapest rates. *Dorms from 2800* • http://nikko-guesthouse.com/en_index.html

Campsites

Nikko has a few campsites a short drive from the station, or a 15-minute walk in the case of Nikko Daiyagawa Park. None currently have English booking available, so ask someone at a tourist information center or prior accommodation to call, if you want to check availability before going. Prices are from around 2000 yen per tent site.

New Kirifuri Campsite (ニュー霧降キャンプ場) - 0288-53-4728 • http://www.kirifuri-camp.com/

Nikko Daiyagawa Park (日光だいや川公園オートキャンプ場) - 0288-23-0201 • https://www.park-tochigi.com/daiyagawa/

Manakanomori (まなかの森 キャンプ) - 0288-21-7748 • http://www.nikko-manakanomori.com/index.html

How to get there and away

From Asakusa station in Tokyo, take a **Tobu Line** Rapid train (2 hours) to Nikko. Free with the passes, or 2798 yen. It's also possible with a JR pass from Ueno station in Tokyo. *Recommended Kanto rail passes: JR Tokyo Wide Pass, Greater Tokyo Pass*

Tourist information (観光案内所)

In JR Nikko station (8am-5:30pm) and Tobu Nikko station (8:30-5pm), as well as 10 minutes up Nihon Romantic Highway from the stations (9am-5pm).

Mount Takao (高尾山)

Autumn colors at Mount Takao

The cheapest and easiest to access mountain and hiking experience near Tokyo city. It really is a great deal, as the one hour train ride costs just 381 yen. There are various trails to take, depending on how much time you want to spend and how much you like to hike. There is also a cable car if you want to cut the journey time to the top in half. Along the way there are plenty of wonderful shrines, parks and nature to keep anyone interested. Casual hikers can take a cable car (8am-5:15pm, adults 480, children 240 yen), while those wanting more of a challenge should skip it and walk up trail #6 (entrance just to the left of the lower cable car station) *Difficulty: Easy to intermediate • Time required: 3-4 hours (take off about one hour if using the cable car)*

Keio Takaosan Onsen Gokurakuyu (京王高尾山温泉 極楽湯)
This brand new hot spring is a great spot to soak your feet and body in after a day of hiking. Includes a sauna and outdoor bath. *1000 yen • 8am-11pm • Behind Takaosanguchi station*

Discount pass: Mt. Takao Discount Ticket

Worth buying if you are sure you will need the cable car at Mount Takao. This ticket includes a return ticket from Shinjuku, plus a return or one-way ticket on the cable car. A 20% saving is given compared to buying separately. Buy at any Keio Line station in Tokyo city, such as in Shinjuku station.

You'll be able to take some amazing photos at Mount Takao, especially during the fall or autumn season. Share them with the world on Facebook, Twitter or Instagram and mention @SuperCheapJapan to help others travel in Japan on the cheap!

Budget food

Keio Takaosan Onsen Gokurakuyu

There is also a Japanese restaurant inside the new hot spring, with a wide choice for all tastes. Curry, soba, sushi, it's got it all. *Meals from 750 yen • 8am-11pm (last order 10pm) • Behind Takaosanguchi station*

Mt. Takao Beer Mount

Beer garden 500 meters up Mount Takao with a commanding view of the mountains, it has to be one of the best in Tokyo and Kanto. Cheap buffet food available, with simple dishes like fried rice, dumplings and pasta. *Drinks from 600 yen, food from 1000-2000 yen • Weekdays 3pm-9pm, Weekends and holidays 2:30pm-9pm • Near cable car upper station*

Water bottle refill spots

There are no water refill spots going up the mountain and the vending machines are a little pricey near the start, so bring plenty of water with you.

Free wifi locations

Keio has free wifi available on the platform of Takaosanguchi station and at Keio Takaosan Onsen Gokurakuyu.

Recommended cheap accommodation

Hikage-sawa Campground (日影沢キャンプ場)

Basic campground, with a simple toilet and just 12 car parking spots. There are no rental facilities. If you can't speak Japanese, get someone at a previous hotel/hostel to call the campsite and check availability beforehand. *FREE • Irregular reception opening times • From Takaosanguchi station, take a Shō futsu (小仏行き) bound bus to Hikage (日影). Show the bus driver to be sure, as well as checking bus times when you arrive as services can be infrequent. You can also hike there in one hour from the summit • 042-663-6689*

How to get there and away

From Shinjuku station, take the Keio Line to Takaosanguchi station (381 yen, 1 hour). You may need to change at Kitano station. The way from Takaosanguchi station is well signposted. *Recommended Kanto rail pass: Greater Tokyo Pass*

Hakone (箱根)

Tokyo's most popular side trip for locals. There is something for everyone here, from hiking to shopping to volcano viewing and hot springs. The town is part of Fuji Hakone Izu National Park, which offers stunning views of Mount Fuji. In addition to this there are lots of standout features such as Owakudani, an eerie volcanic area with lots of yellow fumes, Lake Ashi with its pirate sightseeing boat tour and the Hakone Tozan Train which heads up the mountain. What makes Hakone stand out for budget travelers is the Hakone Free Pass, which offers unlimited transportation in the area and loads of discounts. It really makes Hakone an easy place to get around. Maps and signs are all in English as well, so no chance of getting lost hiking!

Steam rising from Owakudani in Hakone

Discount pass: Hakone Free Pass

The Hakone Free Pass from Odakyu Railway is the best and cheapest way to visit Hakone. It provides unlimited use of the cable car, ropeway, tourist boats, trains and buses in the area, plus the ride from Shinjuku station and back. It also provides discounts or free access to around 50 places in Hakone. Some things in Hakone, especially the ropeway, can get super expensive if you don't have the pass, so it's usually a must buy for budget travelers. You can buy it at the Odakyu Sightseeing Service Center in Shinjuku station or at ticket machines. *Two Day Pass: Adults 5140 yen, Children 1500 yen. Three Day Pass: Adults 5640 yen, Children 1750 yen.*

A little bit of history

At the start of the Edo period, Hakone became a post station on the Tokaido Highway connecting Edo (the old Tokyo) with Kyoto. It became an important checkpoint on the route, which visitors can see a recreation of at the Hakone Sekisho and Checkpoint. Under the strict Tokugawa Shogunate, everyone coming in or leaving was checked and their items inspected by officials. The aim was to restrict the travel of weapons and of women. After the Meiji Restoration, Hakone slowly grew into a fully-fledged town and the Imperial household established a summer villa here, close to the lake. Visitors can also visit this.

Things to do

Owakudani (大涌谷)

A must-see in Hakone, get off at Owakudani station on the ropeway and try some 'kuro-tamago' (black eggs). They have been boiled in the hot spring water, so have black shells! Watch the yellowy volcanic gases blow out of the ground and the fresh hot spring water spew out over the mountain. *FREE • 8:30am-5pm • Owakudani station on ropeway*

Hakone Shrine (箱根神社)

A stunning Shinto shrine complex, starting from a red gate standing in Lake Ashi, running up into the mountain. Apparently founded in 757, the original shrine was said to reside at the summit of Mount Komagatake. It became important for samurai, who would come to pray for luck in their various endeavors. *FREE • 24h*

Hakone Detached Palace Garden (恩賜箱根公園)

The old Imperial family summer house and gardens are now free for you to roam around and take photos of. Walking up into the park gives visitors amazing views over the lake and of Mount Fuji. *FREE • 9am-4:30pm • Onshi-Koen-mae bus stop (route H)*

Hakone Sekisho and Checkpoint (箱根関所)

An authentic recreation of the old trading checkpoint and surrounding village. The people who built this utilized old carpentry and masonry techniques from the Edo period, to make sure everything looks as authentic as possible. *FREE • 9am-5pm • Hakone Sekisho-ato bus stop (route H)*

Sightseeing cruise on Lake Ashi (箱根海賊船)

A rather silly, but amusing way to get across the lake. This 18th century-style ship has been taken over by pirates, like a scene from Pirates of the Caribbean. Especially fun for anyone who likes pirate movies, but a supremely scenic mode of transportation for others! *FREE with Hakone Free Pass or 1000 yen one-way • Togendai, Hakonemachi-ko and Motohakone-ko*

Hakone Open Air Museum (箱根彫刻の森美術館)

A host of very imaginative and thought-provoking statues, sculptures and pieces of architecture, set in a lush, modern garden. The highlight, though, has to be the Picasso gallery, quite a rare collection outside Europe. *1600 yen (1400 yen with the Hakone Free Pass) • 9am-5pm • Chokokunomori station on Hakone Tozan Line • Discounts available at* http://www.hakone-oam.or.jp/

Hakone Gora Park (箱根強羅公園)

Handily located next to a convenience store if you need some more supplies, this park has a western-inspired design. A good place to unwind and have a snack before continuing up the hill. *550 yen (free with the Hakone Free Pass) • 9am-5pm • Koenshimo station on cable car*

Hiking in Hakone

Old Tokaido Highway Hike

An old trading route through the forest to an ancient tea house, this is an uphill but enjoyable hike. Location well signposted from boat port and around, plus buses to take you back after. *Difficulty: Medium • Hike time: 2-3 hours • Moto-Hakone bus stop (routes K, H, Y)*

Around Komagatake and Hakone (駒ヶ岳+箱根山)

There are a few hiking courses around Mount Komagatake and Mount Hakone, which are the main mountains for tourists in Hakone. Note that due to seismic activity, routes can be closed off, so check with the tourism information centers when you get there and ask for their recommended routes. Hiking around Komagatake is an easy to access route, that takes visitors away from all the crowds and tour buses, and into a bit of nature with a closer look at some of the past volcanic activity. *Difficulty: Medium • Hike time: 2-6 hours, depending on route • Owakudani (ropeway) or Sounzan station (cable car)*

Cedar Tree Walk

A nice walk through an ancient cedar avenue, recommended for families or those that want a gentle walk, with no big inclines. *Difficulty: Easy • Walk time: Under 1 hour • Between the Hakone Sekisho and Hakone Detached Palace Garden on the main road. After exiting the carpark of Hakone Detached Palace Garden, take a left and walk down a bit. Entrance is on the right side*

Recommended hot springs (温泉)

Tenzan Onsen (天山湯治郷 ひがな湯治 天山)

Inside a nice hotel, this hot spring has a traditional feel but all the facilities you would expect in a modern spa. *Adults 1300 yen, children 650 yen • 9am-11pm (reception closes at 10pm) • Hakone Tozan (K) bus to Okuyumoto-Iriguchi bus stop. You will see two roads heading off, take the winding road on the left (heading over the river)*

Yunessun (箱根小涌園 ユネッサン)

Not your average hot spring! This rather odd place features baths full of wine, sake or occasionally soda drinks to relax in. A good choice if you have already done an old-fashioned hot spring and want to try something a little crazy. *Adults 2900 yen, children 1600 yen • 9am-7pm • Short walk from Kowakidani station on Hakone Tozan Line*

Hotel Green Plaza (ホテルグリーンプラザ箱根)

Up in the mountains, with open-air baths that offer great views of Mount Fuji. *1600 yen • 1pm-6pm (Mon, Tue, Fri), 3pm-6pm (Wed, Thu), 1pm-3pm (weekends and holidays) • Ubako station on ropeway*

Volunteer guides and tours

Odawara and Hakone Goodwill Guide Club - http://www.ohsgg.com/
Provides volunteer guide services in Hakone and the Odawara area.

Budget food

Eating out is often pricey here and most affordable accommodation comes with a shared kitchen, so most budget travelers should head to a convenience store near Yumoto-Hakone station. Otherwise there are a few reasonably-priced family restaurants near the station, but these do tend to close early. Remember it's legal to drink outside in Japan, so grab a beer from the store and chill out on the river!

Around Yumoto-Hakone station

Kanetsuki (加満幸) - Friendly atmosphere with Japanese set meals and soba, plus curry for kids and big kids alike. Plastic models outside makes it easy to order. *Soba from 600 yen • 11am-6pm • Opposite the station*

Heike (治兵衛) - Another nice joint for some simple hearty Japanese food. *Sets around 1000 yen • 11am-6pm • Further down the shopping street from Kanetsuki, on the left*

Cheap supermarkets (スーパー)

There's not really any cheap supermarket in central Hakone, but there is a supermarket in Odawara (station where your transfer for the train to Yumoto-Hakone station) called Odakyu OX (9am-9:30). Head out the east exit, through the bus terminal to the small triangular park in the road, then take the first right. There is also an A-Co-Op (Aコープ) supermarket near Sengoku bus stop (9am-6pm), to the north west of central Hakone, which you can use the Hakone Free Pass to get to.

Shopping

Gotemba Premium Outlets

The most popular outlet mall for people living in Tokyo or Kanto, Gotemba has all the brands you could imagine. There are more than 200 stores in the complex, plus a food court and Ferris wheel. Prices are at least a bit lower than in the city and tax-free shopping is available. A must for shopaholics. *10am-8pm (Dec to Feb until 19:00) • Free shuttle bus from Gotemba station or take a bus to Gotemba Premium Outlets (included in Hakone Free Pass)*

Recommended cheap accommodation

Hostels and guest houses

K's House Hakone - Onsen Hostel
Cheap hostel chain, but this branch is a little different, with a modern hot spring and new, but traditional looking, architecture. Has a big kitchen with free tea and coffee. *Dorms from 3500 yen*

Guesthouse Azito
Really great prices for private rooms at this guesthouse. This place has a bar to hang out in, plus a kitchen and Japanese tatami floors. *Single rooms from 3500 yen*

Campsites and mountain huts

Lake Ashinoko Camp Village (芦ノ湖キャンプ村)
Located on Lake Ashi (where the sightseeing cruises happen), this campsite is part of Fuji-Hakone National Park. Surrounded by trees, this campsite also has a restaurant, a small shop and a barbeque area. *Tent sites from 1000 yen, car sites from 3000 yen • Reception open 11am-5pm • Near Togendai-ko ropeway station •* http://campmura.com/ *(Japanese only)*

Getting around

The Hakone Tozan Train is a funny little train that takes you on a ride around and up the mountain in a zig-zagging fashion. The Hakone Ropeway and Hakone Tozan Cable car connect visitors with the Lake Ashi from the Hakone Tozan Line, offering stunning views over the mountains. All are included in the Hakone Free Pass, as is an easy-to-use bus network connecting the outlying settlements.

How to get there and away

From Shinjuku, take the Odakyu Line train to Odawara station, then the Hakone Tozan Line to Hakone-Yumoto station (90 mins).

Tourist information (観光案内所)

There is an excellent Odakyu Tourist Center in Shinjuku station, in the Odakyu Department Store building, near the Odakyu ticket gates (8am-6pm). There is also a tourist information center just outside Hakone-Yumoto station (9am-5:45pm).

Kamakura (鎌倉)

Kamakura is a great day trip from Tokyo, and when combined with the Enoshima Kamakura Freepass is a really cheap way to see a more traditional area. Most tourist spots are free or only a few hundred yen (or a somewhat pointless 20 yen for the giant Buddha!). Kamakura is full of interesting shrines, and great for autumn color and cherry blossoms. It can get awfully busy at weekends and on national holidays, so avoid these days if you can.

Discount pass: Enoshima Kamakura Freepass

Provides a round trip to Kamakura from Tokyo (Shinjuku station), as well as unlimited use of trains in the area for one day. There is a lot to do in Kamakura, and most of it is connected by the train lines of this pass. You will therefore start to save money very quickly. The cost of an

Enoshima Kamakura Freepass is about the same as a return ticket. Buy from the Odakyu Sightseeing Service Center in Shinjuku station, or the Odakyu ticket machines in the station. The pass also provides discounts or free gifts at about 20 sites and restaurants in Kamakura. Check http://www.odakyu.jp/english/deels/freepass/enoshima_kamakura/ for the latest on offer. *Adults 1,470 yen, children 740 yen*

The Great Buddha of Kamakura, also known as Daibutsu

A little bit of history

Kamakura, a former capital of Japan, is an ancient city that was once as powerful as Nara and Kyoto. In 1192 warrior Minamoto Yoritomo established the first military government here, the Kamakura Bakufu. Previously the Imperial family in Kyoto held all power. The Hojo clan took over after Yoritomo's death and developed trade in the 13th century, importing Buddhism, Chinese lacquerware and Zen architecture, having a great effect on Japanese society. From the 17th century, Kamakura started to become more important as a temple city. After the war it also prospered as a popular getaway for Tokyoites, with its beaches, resorts and tradition.

Things to do

Daibutsu and Kotokuin Temple (大仏殿高徳院)

World Heritage-listed temple and grand Buddha bronze statue that visitors can walk up into. At a height of more than 13 meters and weighing in at about 121 tons, it's quite a sight. Be sure to have a look around the beautiful garden behind the Great Buddha to get your money's worth. *Adults 200 yen, children 150 yen, Grand Buddha 20 yen • 8am-5:30pm (Apr - Sept), 8am-5pm (Oct - Mar) • 10 mins north from Hase station on the **Enoshima Electric Railway***

Tsurugaoka Hachimangu Shrine (鶴岡八幡宮)

The main shrine in Kamakura, another must see. In 1063, the Minamoto warrior clan created a power base around Kamakura after defeating clans to the north. The leader, Minamoto Yoriyoshi, returned to Kamakura and built this shrine near the coast to give thanks to the gods for his success. The Hachiman Kami (god) is therefore regarded as the protector of the warrior class. The result is a vast complex of well-maintained Japanese shrines, bridges and gardens. *FREE • 8:30am-4pm (24h at New Year) • 10 mins from Kamakura station, east exit*

Hasedera Temple (長谷寺)

Another must see in Kamakura, Hasedera is a significant Buddhist temple. It's said to have been here even before Kamakura was the capital in the Kamakura period (1185-1333). The temple has an 11-faced Kannon statue at around 10 meters tall, which is one of the largest wooden Buddha statues in Japan. The observation platform also has a good view of the town and sea to the south. *Adult 300 yen, children 100 yen (Treasure Museum + 200/100 yen) • 8am-5pm (Mar - Sept), 8am-4:30pm (Oct - Feb), Treasury 9am-5pm (closed Tuesdays) • Short walk from Hase station on Enoshima Electric Railway*

Zeniarai Benten Shrine

Something a little different here as statues and structures are in mini caves, or cut into the rock. Built in 1185 as a place for peace and quiet reflection, Japanese people come here to wash their money and pray for prosperity. Try this if you are a bit 'shrined out', or need somewhere to chill. *FREE • 8am-4:30pm • 20 mins walk from Kamakura station (west exit). Head down the main road leading from the station, through the tunnel, then follow the tourist signs*

Komachi Shopping Street

The main shopping street provides plenty of window shopping opportunities. There are lots of small, cheap Japanese candies to try as well, so as always be on the lookout for free samples! *From Kamakura station, head to the left of the east exit*

Kamakura Beaches

Picturesque beaches with greyish sand and rustic wooden buildings. Popular with surfers, there are stalls where visitors can rent out equipment and beach huts. Note that the beaches get extremely busy in summer. *FREE • South of Yuigahama station on the Enoshima Electric Railway*

Hiking trails

Daibutsu hiking trail

Starting 350m down the road from Kotokuin Temple (signposted), this 3km trail is a nice way to escape the crowds and head up into the forests, passing the odd shrines and temple as you go. *Difficulty: Easy • Hike time: 1-2 hours*

Gionyama hiking trail

Shorter course on the east side, Gionyama also has a cave tomb to explore, in addition to nice views of the city. Considered the easiest hiking trail here. Starts from Myohonji Temple (妙本寺), a five-minute walk from Kamakura station, east exit. *Difficulty: Easy • Hike time: 30 mins*

Tenen hiking trail

Great hike up into the forested hills on the east side. There are several cave tombs along the way, plus this is the best trail to take during the autumn colors season. Most people start at Zuisen-ji Temple (瑞泉寺), 20 mins walk from Kamakura station, east exit (signs may point to Kamakura-gu Shrine first, which is on the way). *Difficulty: Easy • Hike time: 1-2 hours*

Volunteer guides and tours

Kanagawa Systematized Good Will Guide Club - http://volunteerguide-ksgg.jp/

A variety of tours available, such as a 4 hour walking tour to the main sites.

Budget food

On a hot day, getting something cheap from a supermarket or convenience store is best in Kamakura, as it's not as built up as some places. Sadly, the choice of budget restaurants is not as good as back in the big city. But there are still a few cheap restaurants around if needed.

Around Kamakura station
Saizeriya (サイゼリヤ) - Light Italian dishes, such as a small pizza or pasta dish, this is a good spot. *Pizzas from 390 yen, pasta from 399 yen • To the right side of the east exit • 10am-11pm*

Komachi Shopping Street
In addition to the traditional restaurants down this street, there are also some cheap chain restaurants. Expect some tourist prices here, so be warned! The following are in order from Kamakura station (Komachi Shopping Street is the street to the left from the east exit):
Kaiten Misakiko (海鮮三崎港) - Cheap conveyor belt sushi. *Sushi plate from 110 yen + tax*
Komachi Tonkatsu (小満ちとんかつ) - Opposite Kaiten Misakiko, this old school joint has some no fuss Japanese sets. Prices are not great, but this place is a nice way to try everyday Japanese sets. *Japanese sets from 980 yen*
Kamakura Rikyu (りきゅう) - Family run, casual budget Japanese restaurant with decent curries and other favorites. *Curry rice from 500 yen*

Cheap supermarkets (スーパー)
Tokyu Store (東急ストア) is located outside Kamakura station, east exit (9am-10pm).

Shopping

100-yen shops
Daiso (ダイソー) - In the mall to the right side of Kamakura station, east exit. *9am-10pm*

Pharmacy (ドラッグストア)
Hac Drug Kamakura Shop (ハックドラッグ) is near Kamakura station, east exit. Head past the bus terminal, to the main road ahead, then down to the left a bit (9am-9pm).

Recommended cheap accommodation

WeBase Kamakura
Well-run hostel with a variety of rooms to suit most needs. Staff can sort you out with discounted activities and rentals. *Dorm beds from 3800 yen, private rooms from 9600 yen*

Hostel Yuigahama + Soba Bar
Dual-purpose hostels seem to be all the rage. This pleasant old storehouse has been converted into a hostel and soba bar. *Dorm beds from 3500 yen, private rooms from 13000 yen*

Getting around

When you pick up your Enoshima Kamakura Freepass, be sure to take the free sightseeing map. This will show you how to get to each sightseeing spot. All the main sights are well signposted from the stations along this railway and are usually short walks away.

How to get there and away

From Shinjuku station, take the Odakyu Line to Fujisawa station, then the **Enoshima Electric Railway** to Enoshima or Kamakura stations (76 mins, free with Enoshima Kamakura Freepass or 806 yen). The JR line just goes to Kamakura. *Recommended Kanto rail pass: Greater Tokyo Pass*

Tourist information (観光案内所)

Inside Kamakura station (9am-7pm).

Mount Mitake (御岳山)

A 929-meter high, sacred mountain and a great day trip from Tokyo. While Mitake can feel more crowded than other mountains, this is because many locals frequently make a pilgrimage from Tokyo to the shrines up the mountain. There are therefore lots of shrines and religious buildings on the way up, as well as some stunning scenery and lush forest.

Things to do

Hike up for free

As you can see from the picture above, it's an awesomely beautiful walk up. Start from where the Mitake Tozan Railway begins and hike all the way up to Musashi Mitake Shrine. As the hike is not that long, it's best to skip the cost of the cable car and walk all the way up. You'll also see much more of the scenery, as well as mini shrines and religious artifacts. Note there are also extra side-trips that you can hike once you are up the top. For example, the two-and-a-half-hour hike to Mount Otake is well worth it if you have time, as it allows you to escape the crowds a bit. Routes are well signposted, but you can also get a free map at the Mitake Visitor Center at the top. *Difficulty: Easy-Medium • Hike time: 3-4 hours return • Hiking season: Anytime*

Mitake Tozan Railway (御岳登山鉄道)

A traditional cable car that takes visitors from the bottom of Mitake to very near the top. It's only really for those who don't feel up for hiking the whole way up and down. *Adults 590 yen (round-trip 1110 yen), children 290 yen (round-trip 550 yen) • 7:10am-7pm • Located at base of mountain*

Musashi Mitake Shrine (武蔵御嶽神社)

You'll be truly rewarded by this superb example of Shinto architecture once you reach the top. Built by Emperor Suujin in 91BC, the shrine has become a significant spot for the Japanese. There are also a few other shrines dotted around the top, such as Ubuyasusha (産安社), which is used to pray for safe births and healthy children. *FREE • 24h*

Rock Garden (ロックガーデン)

Another worthwhile extension to your hike is to continue to the Rock Garden on the back side of the mountain. You'll see some lovely waterfalls and streams along the way. It's also a good spot to see the autumn leaves. *FREE • Difficulty: Easy-Medium • Hike time: 3-4 hours return from top*

Budget food

Note that there are no cheap supermarkets around Mitake, so it's recommended to bring some food with you to keep costs down. Alternatively, there is a 7-Eleven a minute down to the left after exiting Mitake station, which has a good choice of cheap bentos and sandwiches.

How to get there and away

The cheapest way is to take a JR Chuo Line train from Shinjuku in Tokyo to Ome, then transfer to the Oku-tama bound train and stop off at Mitake (80 mins, 918 yen). Next take the Nishi Tokyo bus to the lower station of the Mitake Tozan Railway (10 mins, 290 yen). *Recommended Kanto rail pass: JR Tokyo Wide Pass*

Kawagoe (川越)

Beautiful, traditional town less than an hour away from central Tokyo, in Saitama prefecture. It features a famous authentic old tower and shopping street, which is why many people call it 'Little Edo' (Edo was the old name for Tokyo). A great place for a nice one-day trip away from the skyscrapers of Tokyo. Kawagoe may not be as popular as other Tokyo side trips, but is still very much on domestic tourism maps.

Discount pass: Kawagoe Discount Pass

From Ikebukuro station in Tokyo, Tobu Railway offers the Kawagoe Discount Pass. It includes a return ticket, plus discounts or complimentary items at various stores in Kawagoe. It's a no brainer. At 700 yen for adults (360 yen for children), it is already cheaper than a return ticket. Available from the Tojo Line ticket offices at Ikebukuro station. The Kawagoe Discount Pass Premium is also available (adults 950 yen, children 480 yen), which additionally includes unlimited bus travel around Kawagoe on Tobu buses, for those that don't want to walk a lot.

Things to do

Toki No Kane Bell Tower (時の鐘)

Still telling the time to residents, this is a traditional watch tower that is often featured in historical dramas. Kawagoe became a castle city in the 17th century (Edo period), and the feudal lord at the time ordered the grand bell tower to keep his subjects informed of the time. Would be crazy not to grab a photo of what is the icon of Kawagoe.

Kashiya Yokocho - Penny Candy Alley (菓子屋横丁)

Founded way back in the Meiji era, Kashiya Yokocho is a stone-paved alley lined with small shops selling nostalgic Japanese candy. Many of the candies are produced using the same processes as in the old days, and visitors can observe this process for free while strolling around. Small portions of these freshly made sweets are available as well, so try a few shops! As ever, keep a look out for free samples and upload your photos to Facebook, Instagram or Twitter. Please mention @SuperCheapJapan when you share with your friends!

Kita-in Temple (喜多院)

A renowned temple only a short walk away from the other points of interest in Kawagoe. First built in 830, it features 540 stone Buddhas with various facial expressions, plus buildings and artifacts from castles in the Edo period. *Adults 400 yen, children 200 yen • Mon-Sat 8:50am-4:30pm, Sundays and holidays to 4:50pm (March 1 - Nov 23); Mon-Sat 8:50am-4pm, Sundays and holidays to 4:20pm (Nov 24 - Feb 28) (closed New Year holidays, Feb 2-3, Apr 2-5, Aug 16) • Down Toshogu Nakain Dori, follow tourist signs*

Volunteer guides and tours

The Kawagoe English Walkers - http://hebbon-juku.com/kawagoe-guide/
Local experts and English enthusiasts, ready to take you around and answer your questions.

Budget food

Wendy's First Kitchen (ファーストキッチン) - Cheap soups, burgers and pasta. *Pasta from 580 yen, burgers from 370 yen • 10am-9pm • Inside Hon-Kawagoe station. Also inside Atre Mall, outside Kawagoe station, east exit*
Hidakaya (日高屋) – Cheap ramen. *From 390 yen • 10am-2am • Outside Kawagoe station, west exit*
Kyotaru (京樽) - Cheap sushi shop. *Sushi from 108 yen • 11am-7pm • Inside Maruhiro Department Store (丸広百貨店), near the east exit of Hon-Kawagoe station*
Ootoya (大戸屋) - Japanese set meals. *Sets from 750 yen • 10am-10pm • Inside EQUIA (エキア) department store, Kawagoe station*
Matsuya (松屋) - Rice bowls and curry. *Gyudon bowls from 290 yen • 24h • Just to the left of Kawagoe station, west exit. Also at Hon-Kawagoe station, east exit*

Cheap supermarkets (スーパー)

There is a large Tobu supermarket in Kawagoe Main (川越マイン), the large building to the right of Kawagoe station, east exit (9am-1am).

Shopping

100-yen shops

Can Do (キャンドゥ) - Inside the Tobu Store complex, outside from Kawagoe station, east exit. *9am-9pm*
Watts (ワッツ) - Inside Hon-Kawagoe station. *10am-8pm*

How to get there and away

From Ikebukuro station (on the JR Yamanote Line), take the Tobu Line to Kawagoe (30 mins, 463 yen or free with Kawagoe Discount Pass). Also possible via the JR **Saikyo Line**.
Recommended Kanto rail passes: JR Tokyo Wide Pass, Greater Tokyo Pass

Tourist information (観光案内所)

Inside Kawagoe station (9am-5pm).

Mount Oyama (大山)

Stunning, secluded pagoda on the way up to Mount Oyama

Along with Mount Takao and Mount Mitake, Mount Oyama is another hiking spot that is cheap to reach from Tokyo. It's a lot less touristy than those two as well, so is recommended for those who want to escape the crowds a bit. The comparative lack of tourists may make it slightly more difficult to get around, but it's still very accessible, especially with the discount pass and help provided by the train company, Odakyu, that takes you there.

The Tanzawa-Oyama area is known for its rich nature and its views of Mount Fuji on clear days. The area is also famous for its autumn leaves. Trails take from two to four hours and can be combined to make even longer routes.

Discount pass: Tanzawa-Oyama Freepass

Another amazing discount pass from Odakyu. This pass makes accessing Oyama, as well as other mountains and hot springs nearby, easy by allowing two days of unlimited bus and train use in the area, as well as the return ticket from Tokyo. The latest information and bus times are all clearly explained in accompanying leaflets. The pass also includes discounts to around two dozen shops, restaurants and museums in the area. You'll still save money if just using for a one-day trip from Tokyo, and it will make traveling so much easier. *From Shinjuku: Ticket A (including the Oyama Cable Car) Adults 2470 yen, children 1230 yen. Ticket B (not including the Oyama Cable Car) Adults 1530 yen, children 760 yen • https://www.odakyu.jp/english/passes/tanzawa_oyama/*

Things to do

Hike Mount Oyama

The main mountain in the area, yet it doesn't tend to get that busy. Adding to the appeal is the fascinating sight of distant shrines as you climb up. The traditional shopping street from the bus stop to the start of the trail is also a perfect photo spot. While there has been some re-routing of the trails recently, it doesn't hamper the experience at all. Be adventurous and try it! *Difficulty: Medium • Hike time: 3-4 hours return (half if using cable car)*

Cable car

If you don't feel like walking the whole way up, then catch a ride on the famous cable car. It departs every 20 minutes and takes visitors on a gentle and highly scenic 800-meter track up to near the top. *Adults 630 yen (round-trip 1110 yen), children 320 yen (round-trip 550 yen) • 9am-5pm • Located a short walk from where the bus drops you off for Oyama*

Hike Mount Hakusan

Combining two of the best things about Japan, hot springs and shrines, this hike has lots to see in addition to the great scenery. Less popular than Oyama, but very quiet. *Difficulty: Medium • Hike time: 3-4 hours return • Get bus from Hon-Atsugi station (check times at Odakyu Shinjuku before)*

Budget food

For the actual hike, get yourself some food from the supermarkets or 100-yen shop listed below. There are also some cheap restaurants around Isehara station for after your hike:

Saizeriya (サイゼリヤ) - Light Italian dishes, such as a small pizza or pasta dish. *Pizzas from 390 yen, pasta from 399 yen • 10am-10pm • Inside shopping mall to left of Isehara station south exit*

Gyouten Ramen (ぎょうてんらーめん) - Tasty tonkotsu (pork based) ramen, with free rice refills. *Ramen from 700 yen • 11am-1am • Head down the road directly ahead of the south exit, then walk to the crossroads. Gyouten is over the crossroad, on the left side*

Matsuya (松屋) - Gyudon and burger eat-in and takeaway. *Gyudon bowls from 290 yen • 24h • Short walk down to the right after leaving from the south exit*

Cheap supermarkets (スーパー)

Odakyu OX is located in Isehara station (9am-10:30pm). Also worth checking out is the Sotetsu Rosen (6am-10:30pm), in the mall to the left after exiting from the south exit of Isehara.

100-yen shops

There is a Can Do 100-yen store in the same mall as Sotetsu Rosen (10am-9pm).

How to get there and away

From Shinjuku in Tokyo, take the Odakyu Odawara Line to Isehara (55 mins, 590 yen). You may need to change along the way at Sagami-Ono or Shin-Yurigaoka. Buses to the mountain usually depart shortly after trains arrive (25 mins, 310 yen). Make sure you also pick up one of the free maps from the Odakyu train station in Shinjuku, which also has the latest track info. *Recommended Kanto rail passes: Greater Tokyo Pass*

Japanese for budget travelers

Essential phrases
Do you speak English? - Eigo ga hanasemas ka? / 英語が話せますか？
Hello! - Konnichiwa! / こんにちは！
Yes - Hai / はい
No - Iie / いいえ
Thank you - Arigatou / ありがとう
Sorry - Sumimasen / すみません
I don't understand - Wakarimasen / わかりません
Please write down (e.g. number, price) - Kaite kudasai / かいてください
Where is the _? - _ wa doko des ka? / _はどこですか？

Insert the following above to ask for directions:
Toilet = Toire / トイレ • Train station = Eki / えき • Subway station = Chikatetsu / ちかてつ

Shopping
How much is this? - Ikura des ka? / いくらですか？
Do you have _? - _ arimas ka? / _ありますか？

Getting food and drink
Do you have an English menu? - Eigo no menyu wa arimas ka? / 英語のメニューはありますか？
I'd like _ please - _ o kudasai / _をください
That please - Kore o kudasai / これをください (point at the item)
Water please (save on drinks) - Omizu o kudasai / お水をください
Refill please! (use if free refills available) - Okawari! / おかわり！
Takeout please - Teiku-auto de / テイクアウトで
Eat-in please - Eeto-in de / イートインで
Is there a cover or table charge? - Chaaji arimas ka? / チャージありますか？

Traveling around
Please tell me when we get to _. (good for buses/trains with no English signs) - _ ni tsuku toki ni oshiete kudasai / _に着くときに教えてください

Numbers
0 - zero / ○
1 - ichi / 一
2 - ni / 二
3 - san / 三
4 - shi/yon / 四
5 - go / 五
6 - roku / 六
7 – shichi/nana / 七
8 - hatchi / 八
9 – kyū / 九
10 - jū / 十
11 – jū-ichi (sound for 10, then sound for 1) / 十一 (so 12 is 'jū-ni', 13 is 'jū-san' etc)
20 - ni-jū (sound for 2, then sound for 10) / 二十 (so 30 is 'san-jū', 31 is 'san-jū-ichi' etc)

Many thanks for reading

Share yourself with the book and win prizes!

Why not share your amazing journey across Japan with your friends by posting a picture on Facebook, Twitter or Instagram? Just include the book (or cover) in the photo and mention @SuperCheapJapan for your chance to win! Monthly prizes will be up for grabs, such as festival tickets, gift vouchers, free stays and much more.

Help spread the word!

Please help the book by writing a review on the website where you bought the book, sharing the book on Facebook or Twitter, or telling a friend. As this is a self-funded indie project, it would be super useful and very much appreciated! It will also allow me to continue to write more budget travel books about this amazing country. Doumo arigatou!

Like or follow us to get the latest tips and deals

Join us on Facebook at https://www.facebook.com/supercheapjapan or follow us on Twitter at https://twitter.com/SuperCheapJapan to receive information on new discounts, the latest deals, cherry blossom forecasts and interesting budget travel reports. You can also get all the latest info at http://www.supercheapjapan.com/.

Picture Attribution

Tokyo pictures ©Tokyo Convention & Visitors Bureau. Mount Fuji © Miles Root. Kawagoe picture Aimaimyi - Own work, CC BY-SA 3.0

About the Author

Super Cheap Japan was written by Matthew Baxter, a British travel author who has lived in and out of Japan for many years. Having traveled across the country for several years, without much money, he has built up an extensive knowledge of budget travel in the Land of the Rising Sun. He now writes professionally for several websites and publications, such as the Japan National Tourist Association, Japan Visitor and All About Japan.

You can contact the author via matt@supercheapjapan.com